A YEAR AND A DAY

Divorce **without** Destruction

Jaime H. Davis, JD
North Carolina Board-Certified
Family Law Specialist

SPARK Publications
Charlotte, North Carolina

A YEAR AND A DAY
Divorce without Destruction
Jaime H. Davis, JD

Designed, produced, and published by SPARK Publications
SPARKpublications.com
Charlotte, North Carolina

Printed in the United States of America
Softcover, January 2020, ISBN: 978-1-943070-72-5
E-book, January 2020, ISBN: 978-1-943070-73-2
Library of Congress Control Number: 2019918068

Disclaimer

While in her role as a lawyer the author's job is to give folks legal advice, the purpose of this book is not to do that. This book is for general informational purposes only, should not be used as legal advice, and is specific to the law in North Carolina. If you have questions, before you take any action, you should consult with a lawyer who is licensed in your state.

Table of Contents

All too often when we think about divorce, we think of *The War of the Roses* — two spouses who will stop at nothing to "win," even if it means destroying the other spouse in the process.

Preface

All too often when we think about divorce, we think of *The War of the Roses*—two spouses who will stop at nothing to "win," even if it means destroying the other spouse in the process. But it doesn't have to be that way. Divorce doesn't have to be destructive.

In 2017, I decided to create a podcast to provide information and tips for getting through a separation and divorce without destroying family relationships or the family finances. Episodes include conversations with divorce-related professionals, such as psychologists, lawyers, and mediators, and cover topics relevant to separation and divorce.

In North Carolina, where I am licensed to practice law, spouses must be separated for a year and a day in order to file for divorce, hence the name of my podcast, *A Year and a Day*. That year is a critical time during which important decisions must be made (either by the spouses or the court) with respect to where the children will live, how the couple's assets and debts will be divided, and how much child support and alimony will be paid.

In large part, this book is based upon episodes of the podcast. As you read the book, please keep in mind that while some of the information presented is universal, laws may differ in other states. If you are contemplating separation, before you take any action you should consult with a lawyer who is licensed in your state.

If you would like to listen to the podcast in its entirety, it is available through Apple podcasts and streaming through my website at divorceistough.com/podcasts.

If you think you might want to separate from your spouse, before ever broaching the subject with them, it is imperative to have a plan in place.

CHAPTER 1

Before You Separate

Marriages end for many reasons. Infidelity, financial stress, growing apart, and even boredom can lead to a separation. When a potential client ends up in my office, most often one of two things has happened: they have decided a separation is in order or have just been told their spouse wants to separate. Either way, making the decision to separate can be life changing, and many myths and misconceptions surround the topic of separation and divorce, making the decision to separate even more difficult. The purpose of this book is to dispel some of those myths and provide tips and guidance for getting through your separation and divorce without destroying family relationships or the family finances.

Have a Plan

If you think you might want to separate from your spouse, before ever broaching the subject with them, it is imperative to have a plan in place. First, make sure you have access to liquid assets and/or credit. Once your spouse is aware you are considering a separation, they may try to restrict your access to funds. It is not uncommon for the supporting spouse to try to starve out the dependent spouse or leverage the fact that the dependent spouse is in a weaker financial position. During the separation, your spouse might not voluntarily provide support, so you may be forced to seek the court's assistance. In such a case, you will need access to funds not only to pay for your living expenses but also to hire the team of professionals necessary to assist with your case.

If you don't already have a separate bank account, establish an account where you can deposit funds that your spouse cannot access. If you and your spouse have a jointly titled bank account, you can take some or all of those funds and deposit them into your separate bank account. Bear in mind this is not free money to you, and you will have to account for it later, but by depositing the funds into your separate account, you will be able to safeguard the money and have access to it in the event your spouse tries to cut you off financially.

If you don't have access to liquid cash, consider any credit that may be available to you, such as credit cards and home equity lines of credit. If you're employed and your paycheck is routinely deposited into an account you hold with your spouse, consider changing your direct deposit so that the funds are deposited into your separate bank account. If you are living in North Carolina and have not yet separated from your spouse, these funds may still be considered marital property and subject to division by the court later, but having access to money now that your spouse can't control may help level the playing field.

Once you have secured access to funds and/or credit, begin securing your team of professionals. In addition to your divorce lawyer, this team is often comprised of a therapist, a CPA, and a financial planner, as well as any professionals you may need to value the marital assets in your case, such as business interests and real estate. If you and your spouse shared the same CPA and/or financial planner during the marriage, but the individual primarily communicated with your spouse, moving forward, you will likely want to find a new professional who is only looking out for your interests and has no allegiance to your spouse.

Gather Your Evidence

In addition to making sure you have access to money, there are several steps you should consider taking prior to discussing separation with your spouse. First, gather documents that will be needed to determine family expenses. These documents often include:

- Five years of tax returns
- Three years of bank statements, including check registers or canceled checks

- Three years of credit card statements
- Recent credit report
- Current balances of all outstanding debts
- Current pay stubs

Next, gather documents that will be needed to determine the distribution of your property. These documents typically include:

- Date of separation and current statements for any bank, brokerage, investment, or other financial accounts
- Date of separation and current statement for any retirement accounts, as well as a statement from the date of marriage if the retirement account existed before the date of marriage
- Appraisals for any real or personal property
- A copy of any homeowner's policy showing insurable value on the contents of any real property
- Five years of corporate tax returns, balance sheets, profit and loss statements, and shareholder agreements if one of the spouses owns a business
- Copies of all insurance policies

Once you have gathered your financial documents, make an inventory of the marital property. Your inventory should include:

- All financial accounts in both parties' name, including account numbers and financial institutions
- All retirement accounts, including account numbers
- All insurance policies on life, health, disability, and real and personal property, including premiums and coverage

It is also a good idea to photograph or video the marital home and contents, as well as any secondary residence and its contents. If personal property begins to disappear, photographs and videos can be helpful to prove what property existed at the time of separation. In addition, if you suspect that your spouse has had or is having an affair, be sure to collect documentation that may evidence the affair. Such documentation can include:

- Detailed cell phone records
- Emails if they can be obtained from a family computer that is used by both spouses and does not require a password unknown to you
- Investigation from a private detective
- Journals, diaries, and daily planners
- Credit card statements

If the phone bill is not detailed, contact the provider and request detailed billing. Also, do not use computer spyware to intercept email messages or attempt to guess the password of a password protected account. This is illegal.

Don't Just Leave

There are a couple of reasons that a spouse should not "just leave" the residence if the spouse decides a separation is in order. The first reason is abandonment. Abandonment is a form of marital misconduct and occurs when one spouse brings the marital cohabitation to an end without justification, without consent, and without the intention of renewing the marital relationship.[1]

In most cases, judges understand that in order for a couple to be separated, someone has to leave the residence; thus, the issue of abandonment is not typically that big of a deal. Usually, the only form of marital misconduct that will bar a dependent spouse from receiving alimony is adultery.[2] How abandonment will affect your particular case, however, depends on the facts specific to your situation, so consult with a lawyer before deciding to separate or move out.

In certain extreme cases, the court may find that one spouse abandoned the other spouse in such an egregious manner that the first spouse should not be entitled to spousal support. For example, in one case[3], the wife told the husband she wanted to move to a new house, and the husband told her he did not want to move. One day when the husband was at work, the wife moved anyway. When the wife moved, she put the husband's clothes on the front porch and in the front yard of their son's house. The husband learned that the wife moved when his friend called him at work out of state. When the husband was finally able to speak with his wife, she told him that she decided to move, she found someone else, and she did not want him anymore. Given these facts, the court found abandonment and denied the wife postseparation support.

Another case[4] in which the court found abandonment involved the following facts. The husband and wife went to Hawaii for a family vacation, and the wife decided to stay three extra days even though the family was supposed to return to North Carolina together. After the family was home for ten days, the wife decided she was going back to Hawaii and purchased tickets using the husband's credit card. The wife told the husband, "I do not know how long I will be gone. If you are here when I get back, that is OK. If you are not here when I get back, then that's OK." The wife

Abandonment is a form of marital misconduct and occurs when one spouse brings the marital cohabitation to an end without justification, without consent, and without the intention of renewing the marital relationship.

then spent two months in Hawaii, continued to use the husband's credit card and even bought a car. Under this set of circumstances, the court found that the wife abandoned the husband. When the court considered the wife's abandonment and the economic factors of the case, it determined that an award of alimony was not appropriate.

Another reason you shouldn't just leave the marital residence is that once you move out of the house, you might not be able to get back in. If you make the decision to move from the marital residence and actually leave the house with your things still in it, you cannot go back to the marital residence to retrieve your personal belongings without the permission of your spouse. If you return to the residence without your spouse's permission or refuse to leave after they ask you to do so, your spouse might call the police, and you might face charges of domestic criminal trespass.[5]

You Don't Need Papers

As a family law practitioner, one of the questions I am most often asked is whether a person needs "papers" to be "legally separated." Contrary to popular belief, in North Carolina, in order to be "legally separated" spouses simply need to live in separate residences with the intent of at least one of the spouses that the separation be permanent. There is no requirement that a document be signed that declares the spouses separated; however, living in separate rooms of the same house or even in separate sides of a duplex is not sufficient. The parties must live under separate roofs.

Couples Counseling

 The "Couples Counseling" section is based on season 1, episode 7, of the podcast with marriage and family therapist Caroline Landen.

Before you make the decision to separate, have you considered couples counseling? In a relationship that isn't going so great, four communication styles may suggest the couple is close to a breakup. In his book *Why Marriages Succeed or Fail,* John Gottman, PhD, calls these communication styles the four horsemen of the apocalypse.[6] These styles are criticism, contempt, defensiveness, and stonewalling. Having these communication styles doesn't necessarily mean the relationship is doomed; it is when these styles become pervasive that they often lead to an end state in a relationship. Criticism involves verbally attacking your partner's person or character. For example, if your partner leaves the toilet seat up, instead of simply saying, "You left the toilet seat up again," you say, "You're such an idiot. Why are you so stupid? You always leave the toilet seat up." These remarks tend to be very personal and attacking in nature and can make it very difficult to have a conversation with your partner.

The second symptom of a relationship that is close to the end is contempt. Contempt puts out the idea that you don't care about your spouse and involves attacking them verbally with the intent to injure or abuse. Whenever your spouse tries to talk to you about anything, you shut down the idea in a disrespectful, mean, and at times abusive way. An example of contempt may be as simple as eye rolling while your partner is expressing their feelings. An extreme example is saying, "You're lucky that you have me. No one else would put up with such a stupid, useless, fat, and ugly person like you. If I divorce you, no one else will ever want to be with you." The goal of contempt is to belittle and deprive your partner of their self-worth.

Defensiveness is the third symptom. Defensiveness is when you are no longer willing to try or feel as if you need to become the victim to protect yourself, and it can manifest itself in different ways. For example, if infidelity is an issue and you're the partner who has been cheated on, you might say things like, "I can yell at you because you had an affair," or "You are the one who screwed up, so I can be angry with you." You are constantly deflecting from yourself and onto your partner, which makes it difficult if not impossible for your partner to say or express anything. Defense is typically a response to criticism, and when we engage in defensiveness, our partners do not feel validated in their concerns.

The fourth and final symptom of a relationship on the rocks is stonewalling. Generally, stonewalling is avoiding or disengaging in response to contempt. But it can also look like engaging in or becoming overly involved in things outside the relationship. In response to contempt, you might walk away, continue doing what you were doing, or change the subject. Or you might be the workaholic partner who overengages at work to avoid engaging at home. Stonewalling generally occurs when a couple is responding to extreme emotional distress and likely accompanies a "fight or flight" response.

When couples use any of these four symptoms as their go-to way of interacting with one another, it can be a sign the relationship is stuck in a pattern that is no longer healthy. In general, there are two main relational patterns. These patterns include a pursuer and a distancer. The pursuer is the spouse who leans into the relationship. During a disagreement, the pursuer wants to talk, and they want to talk right away. The pursuer has a lot to say and a lot of feelings they want to express. Oftentimes, they feel empty and wanting more. Frequently, the pursuer will be the spouse to contact the therapist to start therapy and will generally be the first to talk in therapy.

The distancer on the other hand is most likely withdrawing from the relationship. When the pursuer leans into the relationship, the partner who is a distancer has no room left in the relationship, so they begin to distance themselves. For example, during an emotional conversation the distancer might pick up their cell phone to scroll through Facebook, not listening to anything their partner is saying. At times, the distancer will shut down completely and might resort to stonewalling. The distancer will avoid the issue and try to table it for as long as possible.

Therapy can be a great way for couples to understand these relational patterns. Once a spouse understands that when they exhibit a certain behavior, it causes a reciprocal feeling in their spouse, then they are given the opportunity to do something different. The pursuer can recognize that maybe they need to learn how to contain their anxiety moving forward and that they can't put all those feelings onto their partner. For example, if the pursuer has something they need to request, they should do it directly while avoiding criticism. If the pursuer wants to go on a date night, instead of saying, "We never go on date nights. I really

> **Once a spouse understands that when they exhibit a certain behavior, it causes a reciprocal feeling in their spouse, then they are given the opportunity to do something different.**

Marriage is not a quid pro quo. It is about finding a balance. If the relationship is going to work, both parties need to be careful not to adopt the attitude that they will change only when their spouse changes.

want to go on a date night. Why don't you love me?" the pursuer might consider saying, "I would really love to spend time with you this weekend. Do you have plans Saturday night?"

The crux of therapy is helping the spouses create security with their feelings. For example, the spouse who is the distancer needs to learn how to initiate productive communication with their anxious, pursuing partner, and the way they normally learn to do that is by discovering what their own personal needs are. Distancers tend to attach feelings to the negativity of anger or to minimize and avoid the feelings of sadness, frustration, and fear. In her book *Wanting Sex Again: How to Rediscover Desire and Heal a Sexless Marriage,* therapist Laurie J. Watson challenges the distancers to be affectionate, to underpromise and overdeliver, and to care about the little details.[7] Likewise, therapy can help encourage the anxious pursuing partner to be more seductive. The pursuer needs to be a little bit more mysterious and hold their cards a little bit closer.

Marriage is not a quid pro quo. It is about finding a balance. If the relationship is going to work, both parties need to be careful not to adopt the attitude that they will change only when their spouse changes. Instead, each spouse has to take a risk. They have to trust their spouse enough to get out of the quid pro quo mindset and do something different. Oftentimes, this is easier said than done.

When a client comes into my office and seems unsure about whether they actually want to separate or not, I ask whether they have considered couples therapy. Couples therapy is when two people, who are engaged in some kind of intimate relationship or want to be, enter counseling together, in the same room at the same time. The couple could be dating, married, living together, separated, or even divorced. Anyone who wants to work on their connection can participate in couples therapy.

Couples therapy can seem scary. The idea of being open and vulnerable with a third party in the room is frightening. If you can't talk about your issues with your partner, how is a complete stranger going to help or make you feel comfortable talking through these issues? The role of the therapist is to create a safe place to explore all of the different experiences or narratives the couples have both before they come into therapy and while they are in therapy.

The therapist likely won't offer you any advice, but when you engage in couples therapy, you get information, and you get to spend time with the therapist processing feelings that you may not be used to dealing with outside of the therapy room. The purpose of couples therapy is not necessarily to keep the marriage together. Although often, one partner and sometimes both will claim they want to keep the marriage together, whether because of the children, religious reasons, extended family, or otherwise.

In most cases, the main goal that couples try to work toward in therapy is trying to find congruency. Congruency means whittling down all of the surface interactions of the partners to discover how they really feel beneath the surface. According to John Bowlby and Mary Ainsworth's work with attachment, we all want to know that we matter and that we matter absolutely. Couples therapy is helping each part of the couple see how they want to feel as though they matter and for them to be able to understand how their partner best feels as though they matter.

Therapy can also be useful if one of the partners has unilaterally made the decision to end the marriage. If you do not feel safe at home and you are worried about how your spouse might react to you telling them you want to separate, a therapy session can be a safe place to have this conversation with your spouse. On the other hand, there are some circumstances where communicating the decision to divorce is not appropriate for a therapy session. If the only reason you want to have the conversation about separation during a therapy session is because you are conflict avoidant and want the therapist to be the one to break the news to your spouse, it is probably best if you have the conversation with your spouse at home. Once you have told your spouse that you want a separation, a couples therapy session after the initial conversation can be a good way to process what has transpired and discuss next steps.

Couples therapy can also be helpful after the couple has decided that they are ready to get separated and begin the legal process. The purpose of this type of therapy is to improve communication between the spouses. If successful, the spouses will learn how to talk with each other about what they are experiencing with the divorce process and any areas in which they may be struggling. Unfortunately, the divorce process doesn't always bring out the best in folks, and spouses can quickly get bogged down in the details. I often see this issue arise when the parties are attempting to agree upon a division of their household goods and furnishings. For example, one spouse may have an attachment to a certain piece of personal property such as the wedding china. The wedding china is important to one spouse because it reminds them of a time when the parties were happy and the marriage was good. The other spouse may then decide that the wedding china is important to them too and may want it, but not for the same reasons. A couples therapy session can help the parties talk through these issues and figure out whether they really want the things they think they want. These discussions can help narrow the issues and help the parties better communicate with their respective legal teams, leading to a quicker more cost-effective resolution to their case.

There are two ways spouses can resolve issues arising from their separation: a separation agreement and property settlement or court.

CHAPTER 2 ■

Separation

You've considered everything we discussed in
chapter 1 and decided to separate from your
spouse. But the simple act of separating doesn't
necessarily resolve all of your issues, and it might create
new ones. There are two ways spouses can resolve
issues arising from their separation: (1) a separation
agreement and property settlement or (2) court.

Separation Agreement and Property Settlement

The first way these issues can be resolved is through
a separation agreement and property settlement
(or sometimes simply "separation agreement" as a
shorthand reference). Separation agreements are legal
contracts that can address all of the terms of your
separation, including child custody schedules, child

support payments, property division, responsibility for joint debts, alimony provisions, and any other issues that you and your spouse may have arising out of your marriage. Settlement of disputed issues is almost always preferable to litigation. Resolving your family law issues outside of court is usually quicker and more cost-effective than going to court. If you and your spouse can agree to the terms of your separation and property division, then a separation agreement and property settlement may be for you.

In order to ensure the fairness of a separation agreement, you should make certain all assets, debts, income, and financial liabilities have been fully disclosed by both spouses. If a lawsuit has not been filed, the parties will often participate in a voluntary document exchange prior to a separation agreement being drafted. It is not uncommon for one spouse or the other not to have access to all of the financial information. In such cases, the lawyer for that party will send the other lawyer a list of the financial documents and information they need from the other party to prepare the separation agreement. In addition, the division of assets requires that most assets be valued. Real estate, business interests, tangible personal property, and intangible assets such as retirement benefits may need to be valued by appraisers before a separation agreement can be drafted.

In negotiating what may be an appropriate amount for child support and/or spousal support, both parties should itemize their expenses for at least the last twelve months prior to the separation, also taking into consideration their current expenses. In some cases, accountants are utilized to ensure that there are no unexpected tax consequences to the parties arising from their financial arrangements.

Mediation

"We can't agree," you say. "Looks like we are going to court." Maybe not. Mediation is a process in which a neutral third party, known as a mediator, works with disputing parties to help them explore possible ways to resolve their issues outside of court. The mediator's role is to help facilitate settlement discussions between the parties, but the mediator is not a judge, and they do not get to make the decision about how to ultimately resolve the case. Typically, the mediator comes into the mediation with no information about the case or either of the parties, except for a general understanding of the nature of the issues that will be mediated. Since the mediator is supposed to be a neutral third party, having no information about the case ahead of time can help ensure objectivity, and the mediator will not come into the mediation with preconceived notions about how the case should be resolved.

In family law cases, mediation can be a useful process to help the parties resolve their divorce-related disputes. In fact, in North Carolina, if a party files an equitable distribution claim with the court, mediation of the claim is mandatory; however, the parties can also voluntarily agree to discuss issues related to child custody, child support, and spousal support.[8] One of the benefits to mediation is that it is often quicker and more cost effective than going to court. The parties have more control over how quickly they will attend mediation and how much time and money they will devote to the process.

In addition, mediation gives parties the ability to agree upon a solution that is more tailored to their particular family. Parties who mediate their disputes rather than allowing a judge to decide for them are able to address the fine details of the agreement, such as a more nuanced custody schedule or a creative property settlement. Mediated settlement agreements can include specific procedures for how the terms of the agreement will be performed. Furthermore, because the parties were involved in creating the agreement, there is often a higher likelihood that the parties will actually comply with the terms of the settlement.

In most cases, both parties involved in a mediation have lawyers, but you do not have to be represented by an attorney to participate in mediation. If neither party is represented by counsel, however, the process is slightly different in that assuming you reach a settlement during the mediation, your mediator is prohibited from drafting the document that embodies your agreement. While the mediator can bullet-point his or her understanding of the agreed upon settlement terms, one of the parties will most likely need to hire a lawyer to draft the formal separation agreement or other document that will contain the settlement terms.

It is important to understand that any settlement of your family law issues is not final unless it has been formalized into a valid document that complies with the law. In North Carolina, in order to be valid, separation agreements must be in writing, signed by the parties, and notarized.[9] A verbal agreement or a bullet-point agreement will not suffice. In a typical mediation where there is at least one lawyer involved, that lawyer can draft the document to be signed by both parties, and the deal can be done before everybody leaves mediation that day. The difference with a case where neither party is represented by counsel is that if the parties reach an agreement, they leave mediation with only a summary of the agreement, and their case is not fully resolved.

What kind of mediator do I need?

If you are dealing with the issues arising from a separation, such as child custody, child support, alimony, and equitable distribution, you will want to find a mediator who is a certified family financial mediator. A certified family financial mediator can be a lawyer or a non-lawyer. A certified family financial mediator who is a lawyer must be licensed in North Carolina or elsewhere and have at least five years of legal practice experience. In addition, the lawyer must take a forty-hour training course and demonstrate a basic understanding of family law. In my practice, I generally choose family law attorneys to perform the mediations I attend with my clients because these mediators have a strong background in family law.

They have, in most cases, familiarity with our family court judges and how domestic court works. It can be helpful to getting your case resolved if your mediator has a good understanding of what might happen if the case doesn't settle and ends up in a courtroom in front of a family court judge. The mediator is not supposed to offer legal advice to either party (that's your lawyer's job), but it can be helpful to have another opinion about your case. The mediator can point out to you some weaknesses in your case that you may not have considered, and they can do the same thing with the other side. Having these types of conversations with each party helps bring the parties together and facilitate a settlement because, at the end of the day, mediation is all about compromise. You walk into mediation thinking that you are entitled to something, and the other party arrives thinking they are entitled to the same thing, if not more. Throughout the day, both of you compromise to reach a resolution to your case. Having a mediator who is familiar with the possible range of outcomes can help you through that process.

How do you pick a mediator?

There are several different ways to select a mediator. If you already have a lawyer, you can seek input from your attorney. Since mediation is often required in family law cases, we as family law attorneys represent our clients in mediation quite frequently, and we know who the family financial certified mediators are. We know which mediators do a great job, and we are able to recommend options to our clients. Oftentimes, we will consider the personalities of the parties to determine which mediator will be a good fit. If you do not have a lawyer who can help you select a mediator, another way to find a mediator is through the North Carolina Dispute Resolution Commission's website where they keep a list of certified mediators.[10] The list of mediators can be searched by name and also by the type of law the mediator practices. Mediators who are certified as family financial mediators will be designated as such on the website.

How long does mediation last, and how much does it cost?

Mediation typically lasts a lot longer than you might think. A really efficient mediation with just a few issues might last four or five hours. More complicated cases—where you are negotiating child support, the division of your property and debt, and whether one person owes the other any spousal support—can last ten to twelve hours or more, and sometimes you don't finish the mediation in one day and have to schedule a second day to reconvene.

With respect to the cost, a mediation that leads to a resolution of the case or at least a narrowing of the issues is far less expensive than having a trial. In North Carolina, most family financial mediators charge an hourly rate that can range from $150 an hour to $300 per hour or more. Most mediators also charge a small administrative fee, usually about $150 or $175. For example, if the mediation lasts five hours and the mediator charges $200 per hour with a $150 administrative fee, the total cost will be $1,150 or $575 per person. In most cases, the parties divide the cost of that mediator's fees equally.

All things considered, mediation is usually a fairly cost-effective way to resolve a case, especially if you hire a mediator with a reasonable hourly rate and both sides are prepared for the mediation. If you go into the mediation session not having done your homework, the mediation will likely last longer. In my practice, I try to have a first settlement offer prepared by the time I get to mediation to help streamline the process. Overall, it just depends on how many issues you have to work out. Some of these financial issues can take a significant amount of time to resolve because the devil is in the details. If you are trying to divide multiple financial accounts, decide who is going to take on multiple credit card debts, and figure out who will keep the house or whether it will be sold, it takes time to work through all of those issues.

When is mediation over?

If the parties are represented by counsel and they reach an agreement, in most cases mediation is over when the settlement documents are signed. Some exceptions exist, and sometimes documents shouldn't be signed that particular day. For example, if mediation lasts late into the evening, the parties may wish to take some additional time to review the settlement documents. However, for those cases where the parties are unable to reach an agreement and the mediator declares an impasse, when exactly mediation will end depends on the particular case. There usually comes a time in the mediation process where people become locked in their positions and stop making movement toward resolution despite any "business-decision conversations" that I or the mediator might have with the party.

A "business-decision conversation" involves talking with the party about the cost of court versus the issue about which the party doesn't think they can further negotiate. For example, if the parties are $5,000 apart and if my client isn't willing to make any further concessions, I will have a conversation with the client explaining if they leave mediation without a settlement, the client will likely pay far in excess of $5,000 to take the case to court. The client can then decide whether to forgo or to pay the $5,000 (whichever the case may be) and have a firmly done deal, or to pay his or her lawyer a lot more than $5,000 to roll the dice and go to court.

Sometimes, however, it isn't that simple, and parties aren't in disagreement about a sum of money that can be quantified, but rather they don't agree on what custodial schedule will work best for their children. Having a "business-decision conversation" can be difficult, if not impossible, to have with clients when they are at odds over a custody schedule. If a parent becomes really entrenched and believes that their proposed custody schedule is what's in the best interest of the child, and the other parent disagrees, it can be difficult to get the person to move from their position.

Another situation that can be difficult to resolve in mediation, or otherwise, involves custody cases where there is a relocation or one parent lives very far away from the other parent. If both parents want primary custody of the child, there is not a lot of room for compromise when the parties live far from one another. If the decision to be made is whether the parent is going be allowed to move to whatever state they want to go to, or whether he or she will have to stay in North Carolina, the case becomes an all-or-nothing scenario. When counseling my clients, I often talk to them about the possible range of outcomes if their case proceeds to court. What does your best day in court look like versus your worst day in court? If you agree to a relocation and you are the person who doesn't want the child to move, then you would be in essence agreeing to your worst day in court.

While it may seem that these types of cases might not be ideal for mediation, the mediator may be able to help offer some creative solutions for compromise. Sometimes when parties and lawyers have become entrenched in their positions, having a neutral person with a fresh perspective and creative ideas can sometimes resolve seemingly unresolvable problems.

Is mediation right for every case?

With all of its benefits, mediation is not right for every case. Unlike a courtroom setting, mediation typically has very few rules. This lack of formality can be great for promoting settlement, but in cases where one party is timid and the other party is more vocal and aggressive, the timid party runs the risk of not getting everything to which they might be legally entitled because they are unable to assert their position. Having a lawyer present during the mediation to represent your interests can help mitigate this problem, but in some cases—particularly when domestic violence is involved—mediation may not be appropriate. In such cases, mediation may just perpetuate the power imbalance and provide another way for the abuser to harm the victim if the victim is not comfortable asserting their position.

Finally, there is no guarantee that mediation will be successful and that the parties will reach an agreement. If mediation is not successful, the parties may have to go through the time-consuming and expensive process of trial after already having spent time and money to prepare for and participate in mediation. While mediation might not be the best course of action in every case, because of its potential benefits, mediation is an option that should at least be considered. If you have questions about whether mediation would be appropriate for your case, you should consult with a family law attorney.

Court

If you are unable to agree upon the terms of a separation agreement and property settlement with your spouse, or if your spouse simply will not participate in the process, your final option is to file a lawsuit and seek the court's assistance. Most often, the claims that are filed include child custody, child support, postseparation support, alimony, and equitable distribution. Each of these claims will be discussed in further detail in the chapters that follow. Bear in mind that filing a lawsuit does not mean you will necessarily have to go court as most family law cases settle at some point before the final hearing.

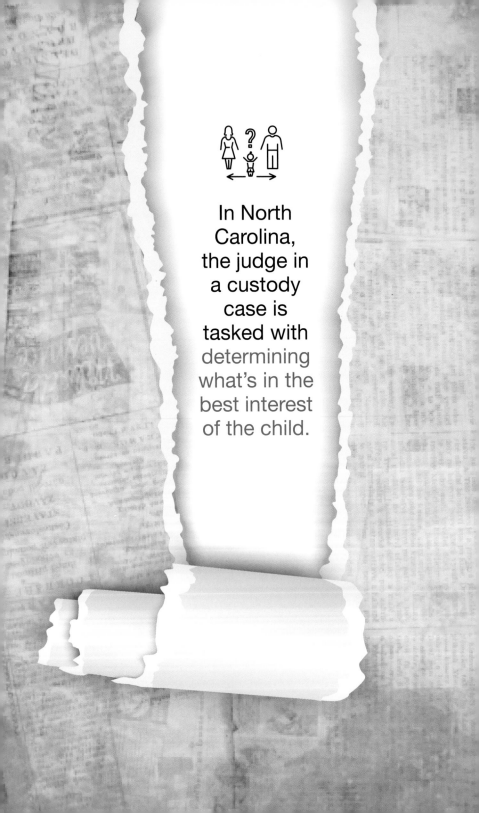

In North Carolina, the judge in a custody case is tasked with determining what's in the best interest of the child.

CHAPTER 3

Child Custody

In an ideal world, parents don't separate, or if they do, they do it amicably and are able to agree upon the custody of their children. However, sometimes, despite using your best efforts, you might find yourself in the middle of a custody lawsuit. This chapter will discuss some tips and offer guidance if you find yourself involved in a child custody case. One of the most important things I tell my clients who are involved in custody cases is to remember it's not about you or what you want. It's about what is best for your children.

Navigating Your Custody Case

 The "Navigating Your Custody Case" section is based on season 1, episode 11, of the podcast with my colleague and fellow family law attorney Melissa Essick.

In North Carolina, the judge in a custody case is tasked with determining what's in the best interest of the child. So when you are out in the real world trying to make a decision as to what custody schedule you want to implement or want to suggest for your children, you need to look at the specific needs of your children. Do your children have special medical needs? Do they have any learning disabilities? Do they participate in a lot of extracurricular activities?

Custody schedules come in all shapes and sizes, and if the parents can agree, they can craft a schedule that is tailored to their specific family. A custody schedule can be 50/50, meaning that the parents spend equal time with the children, but how a 50/50 schedule looks can vary from family to family. For example, parents may choose to implement a 2-2-3 schedule. With a 2-2-3 schedule, the children spend Monday and Tuesday with one parent, Wednesday and Thursday with the other parent, and the parents alternate the weekends. Whichever parent did not have custodial time with the children during the weekend, will have custody of the children the following Monday and Tuesday and the rotation will continue from there. Similar to the 2-2-3 schedule is the 2-2-5 schedule. If parents choose to follow a 2-2-5 schedule, the children will spend every Monday and Tuesday with one parent, every Wednesday and Thursday with the other parent, and the parents will alternate the weekends. A benefit to this schedule is that the children know that they will be with the same parent on the same weekdays every week. A downside to this schedule is that each parent will have to go five days without seeing the children when it is the other parent's weekend to have custodial time. Finally, a third variation of a 50/50 custody schedule is week-on/week-off. As the name implies, if a family follows a week-on/week-off custody schedule, the children will spend one week with one parent, the next week with the other parent, and the schedule will continue to rotate from there.

In some cases, a 50/50 schedule may not be feasible for one reason or another. A parent's work travel schedule may prevent them from exercising equal time with the children, or a parent may be unfit to have equal time with the children for some reason. In those cases, the custody schedule will typically be some variation of an every-other-weekend schedule, meaning that the children will reside primarily with one parent and visit with the other parent every other weekend and maybe a dinner visit or overnight during the off-week. The length of the weekend can vary from case to case. In some cases, the weekend will begin on Friday after school and last until Sunday evening. In other cases, the weekend will begin on Thursday after school and last until Monday morning when the children return to school. Some families prefer custodial exchanges that occur at school rather than at a parent's residence because such exchanges help reduce conflict and in turn alleviate anxiety for the children.

Sometimes, a schedule that both parents think will be in the child's best interest doesn't end up working out, because the schedule does not meet their child's particular needs. For example, the parents agree on a 50/50 custody schedule where their daughter spends Mondays and Tuesdays with one parent (let's say mom), Wednesdays and Thursdays with the other (let's say dad), and then they alternate the weekends. On mom's days, mom picks the daughter up from school, and on dad's days, dad allows the daughter to ride the bus home from school. The daughter in this case has a learning disability, and after the parties start this particular custody schedule, she begins having serious issues with focusing and getting her schoolwork done. The inconsistency in how the daughter goes home from school begins affecting her school performance. Ultimately, the parents decide it is best for their daughter to have a very strict routine during the week. Rather than changing their overnight schedule, they agree to allow the daughter to ride home on the bus every day so that she has a consistent routine. Even on mom's days, the daughter would ride the bus home to dad's house and do her homework, and mom would pick her up there. This example is one of many that illustrates why you need to consider the specific needs of the child and not necessarily just making sure that mom and dad have equal time with the child.

Interacting with the Other Parent

In some cases, parents simply cannot agree upon a schedule for their children and they have to seek the court's help to determine a schedule. For parents who find themselves involved in custody litigation, it is important to be cordial and respectful to the other parent. You are obviously going through a divorce for a reason, and there are probably some hard feelings, one way or the other; that's understandable. However, the child does not need to be a witness to those negative feelings. The child needs to know that both parents respect one another. Whenever you see the other parent in the presence of your child you can say hello. You don't have to get into the details of whether the child support is being paid or the details of who is picking up the children when. Be cordial and allow those other types of communications to take place outside the presence of the children. You can email, text or call the other parent about these other issues, but don't address them when in the same setting as the child.

Can I send messages through the children?

I can't stress enough the importance of not sending messages through your children. If you have something to say to the other parent, send them a text message or an email, but don't tell your son or daughter, "Hey, would you mind asking your mom X, Y, or Z?" Asking your child to relay a message to the other parent places your child squarely in the middle of what should be an adult conversation. A lot of times, this issue will arise if one parent has not paid the other for something. For example, mom might ask the child, "Will you ask dad when he's going to pay me back for your baseball registration?" or the child may ask his dad to sign him

When you are involved in a custody case, assume that everything you write is going to be read by a judge whether you are writing to your child, the other parent, or to a third party.

up for baseball, and dad tells him, "Sure, if you ask your mom to pay for it." These types of communications with the child place him in a very uncomfortable position and should not occur.

There may be a need to vary from the custodial schedule even after a custody order is entered or an agreement is reached; however, the child doesn't need to be the one asking permission of the other parent to change the schedule. If a parent needs to vary from the set schedule, he or she needs to ask the other parent first. The parents need to agree upon any changes to the schedule before the child is made aware that there may be a variation in the schedule. For example, dad wants to take the children to Disney World, but part of the trip will overlap with mom's time. Dad should first ask mom whether she will agree to vary the schedule to accommodate the trip rather than saying to the child, "I would love to take you to Disney World if your mom will let me."

How should I communicate with the other parent?

In many cases, parents going through a divorce have difficulty communicating with one another face to face or over the telephone. In those cases, the majority of their communications are in writing, either by email or text message. When you are involved in a custody case, assume that everything you write is going to be read by a judge whether you are writing to your child, the other parent, or to a third party. Be respectful and cordial in your written communications and make sure that if a question is asked that needs a response that you are in fact responding to the question. Sometimes a parent doesn't want to communicate with the other parent because of the adult issues that are going on in their relationship; however, if the parent asks a question, whether it is about an extracurricular activity or mental health treatment for the child, you need to respond to the question in a timely manner and do so respectfully.

I often tell my clients if they receive an email from the other parent, and it addresses three or four different issues, I will advise them to number their responses accordingly—1, 2, 3, and 4. Even if the answer to the question is just "OK," you should type out the word "OK" so that the other parent knows you read the question, that you are OK with whatever the issue is, and that the other parent knows they have permission to do whatever it is they are asking to be able to do with the child. In addition, don't use email or text messages as a way to take a jab at the other parent. If you are communicating about the children, keep it to issues related to the children, and if you need to, talk to your therapist about those other personal things that you might think about the other parent.

What information should I share?

During the marriage, one parent or the other may have been the parent who primarily signed the kids up for activities and was on all of the email lists to get the soccer schedule or the ballet recital information or whatever the activity was. After a separation, it is important that both parents have access to this information. My advice is to share as much information about the children's activities as you can with the other parent. It is better to overshare than not to share at all. Make sure both parents are on the email lists for all the extracurricular activities. Share both parents' contact information with the coaches. In addition, share both parents' contact information with the children's schools and medical providers. When you are filling out intake forms at the doctor's office or for school registration or whatever the activity may be, you need to make sure that you list the other parent's contact information on the form along with your own. These documents are very easy to obtain and oftentimes are used in trial to show that one parent is trying to control the flow of information about the children by not including the other parent's contact information. If you think you are going to pull one over on your ex-spouse by not including their information, think again. When given the option, take the high road. If the other parent continually asks you for the details of the children's activities or schedule, and you know they have gotten this information before, just give it to them again. It can only serve to benefit your child. You do not want your son or daughter feeling like mom or dad neglected them or forgot to show up for their preschool graduation or their soccer tournament. Share the information for the sake of your child. You don't want your child to be disappointed if their other parent is not there, and you certainly don't want to be the reason for the disappointment.

How should I communicate with the children?

As with all of your written communications when you are involved in a custody case, assume if you are communicating with your child in writing that you will see it again. If you are texting your child, you may think the messages are private between you and your child, but there is a chance that the text message could come up again in court. Also, be mindful that you are not interrogating your children. Ask your child about his day or what fun things he did with the other parent, but don't use your child as a way to gather information about the other parent. Your child will pick up on what you are trying to do. Limit your conversations with your child to things that are about them.

Also, keep in mind the age of your child when you are insisting on a certain form of communication with him or her. Given the technology available today, many parents want to have FaceTime calls with their children. Frequently, especially with small children, they do not want to talk on the phone. It is nothing against the parent, but the child would rather play or do whatever else they might be doing rather than talk to the other parent. Be mindful of the number of times you contact the child when the child is with the other parent and also the duration of the call. Keep it short and don't take it personally. Your child doesn't love you any less.

The time of day you call your children when they are with the other parent is also important. Call at a time that is going to be convenient for both the child and the other parent, and again, it all comes back to being respectful and courteous. Don't call during the middle of dinner. Evenings can be busy with little ones, so check with the other parent and see what works for them and their household. For example, if you know the other parent is going to be at the pool with the children on Saturday afternoon, don't call at that time because most likely the child is not going to want to talk to you, and it's going to put the other parent in a difficult situation.

Also, consider giving your child privacy for their calls with the other parent. If a child is old enough, they will naturally step away from you when they receive a phone call from the other parent, but if a child is younger and not necessarily as familiar with the phone, it may be more comfortable for them to talk on a speakerphone. Even in those situations, I encourage my clients to allow the child some privacy. Let the child go into the playroom and close the door if that's an option. The idea is to make sure that the child feels comfortable speaking freely with the other parent, and the other parent doesn't feel like you are monitoring their calls with the child. Remember that you will want the same respect when the child is with the other parent.

Finally, be mindful that you are not inadvertently disparaging the other parent in front of the child. Offhanded remarks such as "your dad is running late again," can be damaging to the child because you are putting the child in a position of having to form an opinion about whether or not something is really dad's fault. These types of remarks can also make the child somewhat defensive of the other parent, which can put the child in an uncomfortable position. When in doubt, just be fact-based with your child. Eventually, the child might take all of these offhanded remarks cumulatively, and whether you intended to or not, you could cause your child to feel alienated from the other parent. If you really need to know information that you can't get from any source other than your child, just ask the question that you want the answer to without implying some underlying negative inference about the other parent.

Can I still use social media?

When you are involved in a custody case, the best course of action is to stay off of social media to the extent you are able, but if you can't completely give up social media, be mindful of what you're posting. Social media posts can be used as evidence in court to show which people you are associating with or the times that you are out and about, especially if you are out with your children. Particularly for social media sites that allow you to share your location and "check in" to places, the court can see exactly what you are doing, when you're doing it, and with whom. Pictures

The best course of action is to stay off of social media to the extent you are able, but if you can't completely give up social media, be mindful of what you're posting.

of partying or copious amounts of alcohol being consumed, especially if the children are in the pictures with you, are not a good idea. Once you are involved in a lawsuit or if a lawsuit could be imminent, you have a duty to preserve evidence, and that means you can't go into your social media accounts and just cherry pick things to delete. It all has to stay there—the good, the bad, and the ugly. So when in doubt, don't put it on the Internet.

In addition, it can be tempting to post to your social media accounts about what you are going through and the emotions you are experiencing following a separation. Don't do it. In addition to these posts potentially being used against you in court, ultimately, your children will get to an age where they will be able to read those comments. Also remember that sarcasm doesn't necessarily come through on social media, and the possibility exists that the other parent or the court is going to take something you said on social media quite literally, and if taken literally and negatively, it might damage your custody case.

What if I make a mistake?

You have to remember that the stuff you post on social media is out there, and when you are involved in a lawsuit, odds are good you are going to see some of it again. When asked about it later at your deposition or in a court hearing, don't lie about it. You will get caught. When you are in court, you can highlight your own positive qualities, but don't lie about your past weaknesses or what you have put on social media. The other lawyer is going to impeach you with this information. They are going to have the picture or the post or the email or the text message, and they are going to show it to you in front of the judge. If you have already lied about it, and they prove that you were lying, you are going to lose credibility with the court.

You need to be able to acknowledge your parenting mistakes. We, as parents, have all made mistakes, and we all have our own weaknesses. If you are in a deposition or in court, and the opposing counsel asks you what your parenting weaknesses are, and you can't think of one thing that is a weakness, it simply isn't true, and you will lose credibility with the court. It is OK to make mistakes and acknowledge them and explain to the court how you wish you had done things differently and that you learned from the experience. Another common question that lawyers ask in custody cases, for example, if the child is having difficulty in school, is, "What responsibility do you take for this situation?" When the parent says none and tries to blame it all on the other parent, it's just not believable. Similarly, if you're asked about the other parent's strengths, you need to be able to list a few because the other parent most likely has at least one or two strengths. It's OK to acknowledge that the other parent has strengths and that you have weaknesses. Be honest. People get in trouble when they overstate things. When you have been asked about the other parties' strengths and the only thing you can think of is that the other parent loves the children, it isn't believable, and it doesn't help your custody case.

How involved can my new significant other be with the kids?

When you are involved in a custody case, the court will consider your living arrangements, so don't be too quick to move in with your new significant other. Among other things, the court will consider the environment of the home, whether or not it's safe and stable, and whether the child has proper living accommodations. Did the child have their own bedroom when you were living with the other parent? Does the child have their own bedroom at your new residence? Also be mindful of the person with whom you are associating. The judge will be making a determination about what's in your child's best interest, and if your new partner has a criminal background, for instance, or is associating with dangerous individuals, the judge is going to consider that fact when making a ruling as to whether or not it is appropriate for the child to be around your new significant other.

Also be aware that if you are spending all of your custodial time with the significant other rather than spending one-on-one time with your children, the judge may not consider your actions to be in the best interest of your children. The judge is going to want to see that each child is getting individual love and attention. If you are spending 100 percent of your time with the significant other, odds are good your children are not getting the individual attention they need. When entering into a new relationship, be sure it is with a person who is suitable to be around your children and be mindful that you are not spending too much time with this person to the detriment of your children.

Conversely, if your ex-spouse has been dating someone for a long period of time and that person is good to your child, it is important to try not to be jealous of that person or to feel threatened by the relationship that this new significant other has with your child. The more people who love or care for your child, the better. This new significant other is not going to replace you as a parent. This is just another person who can be a positive influence on your child.

When is it over?

You have just made it through your three-day custody trial, the judge has made a ruling, and you walk out of the courtroom thankful the whole ordeal it is over. Unfortunately, with custody issues, it is never truly over. The litigation may be finished for now, but in North Carolina, either parent can file a motion to modify custody if there is a substantial change in circumstances affecting the welfare of the child until the child turns eighteen years old.[11] So there is always a chance that another motion could be filed in the future, and you might find yourself back in front of a judge. Given the possibility that a motion to modify custody might be filed, even after the custody order is entered, be mindful of your written communications with the other parent and continue to follow the "rules" discussed in this chapter. You may want to continue keeping a journal of things that happen related to the children and keep track of the number of overnights that the other parent was supposed to have with the children but didn't exercise.

Additionally, even after your child turns eighteen, you and your ex are going to be your child's parents for the rest of their life, which means you will have to see and be in contact with the other parent. Hopefully, you will foster a relationship with the other parent such that you can be in the same room and be cordial to one another. You will continue to see your child's other parent at graduations and weddings and for the births of your grandchildren. You want that time for your child to be about your child and not about your relationship with the other parent.

Handling the First Holidays Following Separation

The first holiday season after a separation can evoke a variety of emotions for both you and your children. Steeped as they are in memories and traditions, the holidays are likely to stir up feelings of fear, stress, and potentially even sadness. The following tips offer guidance for you and your children to prepare for and cope with these emotions as you enter your first holiday season as a separated/divorced family.

First, acknowledge that this year will be different. Memories of seasons past are bound to arise. Show your children that it's OK to reminisce about the past by doing so yourself in a positive way. In addition,

> **Typically, parents handle the holidays in one of two ways: either by alternating years (where dad has odd years, and mom has even years, or vice versa), or parents share the actual holiday itself.**

recognize that this may be the first time your children are spending a major holiday, or part of a major holiday, away from the other parent. Depending on how long you've been married, it has likely been many years since you've spent a holiday alone. Know that it's OK to feel sad and perhaps even angry, and let your kids know this too. Then reassure them (and yourself!) that although this season will be different, it can still be enjoyable.

Have a plan. Knowing in advance how you and your ex-spouse are going to divide the time with your children—and sharing that plan—gives everyone time to adjust to the "new normal." It may also be a good idea to share that plan with extended family. Most people spell out holiday arrangements in their separation agreements. Typically, parents handle the holidays in one of two ways: either by alternating years (where dad has odd years, and mom has even years, or vice versa), or parents share the actual holiday itself. For example, one parent might have the children on Christmas Eve and Christmas morning, and the other parent would then have the children from Christmas afternoon through December 27th. The latter schedule usually alternates every other year as well. When deciding how to share the holidays with your co-parent, keep the best interests of your children in mind. If carving up the holiday is too disruptive for the kids, perhaps it's best to celebrate with them on another day. After all, the date on the calendar matters less than ensuring you celebrate the holiday with your loved ones.

Talk with your ex about gifts for your children. In addition to lessening the chances for duplicate gifts, talking with your ex about holiday gifts will hopefully prevent disappointment or, on the other end of the spectrum, overindulgence. You should also consider helping your children select a gift for the other parent. This gesture will help show your children the true meaning of the season and let them know it is OK for them to celebrate the holiday with both of their parents.

Preserve traditions. If your children always attend Thanksgiving dinner at their paternal grandparents' house, it's probably best to let them continue that tradition. In addition, particularly if your children are young, you might consider having Santa Claus visit both homes.

Know how you'll spend your alone time. When your children are with their other parent, consider spending time with friends and family. Visit relatives or host a brunch for friends, or use your time before the children arrive productively, decorating the house, preparing meals, and getting gifts ready. If this is your first Thanksgiving alone, you might opt to shop the Black Friday sales or start pulling out your winter holiday decorations. Signing up to deliver holiday meals to seniors can be a great way to spend your time with someone who is also spending the holiday alone. Finally, you might wish to use your time for self-care: take a bath, read a book, or watch a favorite movie. Whatever you do, have *something* to do. Planning ahead will help ensure that you don't leave yourself in a position where you're walking around your house aimlessly missing your children.

Finally, create new traditions. Divorce is a new chapter in your life. While preserving the traditions of earlier years, it's also an opportunity to fill the season with new traditions. Whatever those traditions may be, allow them to capture the true essences of the holiday season: gratitude, hope, and joy.

Co-parenting Therapy

 The "Co-parenting Therapy" section is based on season 1, episode 1, of the podcast with special guest Lori Thomas, JD, PhD.

Clients often ask how they can possibly continue to parent their children with a former spouse that they no longer trust or get along with very well. On the first episode of the podcast, I had the unique opportunity to discuss the issue of co-parenting with

Lori Thomas, JD, PhD, a licensed psychologist who specializes in the treatment of children and adolescents. According to Dr. Thomas, one of the key factors to effective co-parenting is creating boundaries between the personal relationship issues that the couple had prior to their separation and their co-parenting relationship moving forward. The parents must put aside their personal differences and have a joint investment in their child.

Co-parenting after a separation does not always come naturally, but there are ways to learn effective co-parenting. Developing better communication is a way to begin effective co-parenting. Parents are going through a difficult time postseparation, and usually, a lot of history led up to the separation. Even if the parents had good communication prior to the separation, there is a tendency to withdraw from that communication once the parents separate. Co-parenting therapy can help parents rebuild that communication by teaching them the dos and don'ts for how to communicate with the other parent following separation.

For example, when communicating with your child's other parent following a separation, stay focused on just the issues relating to the child and not what your partner did or didn't do in the marriage in the years leading up to the separation. Divorce is a loss for many people, not unlike the death of a loved one, and the stages of grief you experience can be similar. There will be different phases in the process for parents being able to communicate with each other.

According to Dr. Thomas, evidence suggests that parents who had more commitment to each other and investment in working together to raise their children prior to the separation are more likely over time to show better ability to parent together in the future.[12] Parents who had a poor-quality relationship prior to the separation are likely to struggle with communicating about their child following the separation.[13] Co-parenting therapy can offer a safe place for the parties to try to find some common ground where they can communicate about their children. The therapist can help the parents start where they have common agreements about what they want for their children, and then help them build on those common values moving forward in their communication and relationship to one another.

> **One of the key factors to effective co-parenting is creating boundaries between the personal relationship issues that the couple had prior to their separation and their co-parenting relationship moving forward.**

What are the benefits of co-parenting therapy?

Successful co-parenting has many benefits for the children and the stability of the family. Divorce can be challenging for families because of the many changes, whether those changes are in terms of resources (less money to go around) or in terms of changes in living environments (the children may be going between two new homes). There is good evidence to suggest that if parents can be successful in their co-parenting relationship, they will help their children's emotional and social development.[14] For example, the noncustodial parent may be more likely to be involved in the parenting of the children if there is less strife between the parents and they can work together to be successful co-parents. In addition, successful co-parenting has been linked to better behavioral outcomes.[15] According to Dr. Thomas, "Children behave better. There's research to suggest that the first year following a separation is the hardest adjustment year for kids because there is so much change and transition and that the children's academics might be affected. But we know that if the parents can work on successful co-parenting, some of those differences are mediated or buffered by the parents being able to manage their children in a collaborative way."[16]

Is co-parenting therapy right for everyone?

Many factors support successful co-parenting. According to Dr. Thomas, one of those factors includes how much of a relationship the parents had prior to separating. If the couple was not together for a long period of time, married or not, and there was a separation right after the birth of the child or soon after, it may be more difficult for those parents to be successful at co-parenting. Another factor Dr. Thomas points to is the personality of the child. The child may have some serious behavior problems that can make it difficult for parents to successfully co-parent because they have the strain of their relationship plus the strain of managing the difficulties of the child. With that said, however, in general, many people can benefit from co-parenting therapy.[17]

There are some basic things parents can benefit from hearing and working on together. Even if the parents may not be the best communicators with one another, co-parenting therapy may help them focus and think about having their communications be about the child for the benefit of the child. Despite the benefits of co-parenting therapy, some people remain resistant. "It is an emotional time," said Dr. Thomas, "particularly if they have been really invested in the relationship and their relationship is now ending. Usually, it can be really difficult to be in the same room with the person who hurt them emotionally." In addition, infidelity in a relationship can make it difficult for the parties to trust each other in parenting decisions, and the mental health or mental health problems of one party can affect the relationship in terms of parenting. For example, said Dr. Thomas, "There are some things that couples will accept about one another when they're married, but once they get separated, it becomes more of an emphasized issue. The parent begins to concentrate on what he or she ideally wants to have for the child now that the parents are separated because he or she was not able to provide that for the child prior to separation."

How can I improve my co-parenting skills?

Co-parenting therapy isn't for everyone, but there are some basic tips parents can follow to improve their co-parenting skills. First and foremost, said Dr. Thomas, "Parents need to realize that they don't have to be perfect. Parents don't have to be perfect co-parents. They don't have to be perfect parents. They just need to be good enough." In addition, thinking about basic things like keeping your focus on the child, keeping your cool, and if you think you are going to lose your cool by having in-person communications, then trying the more passive communication vehicles like email can help. Dr. Thomas advises not criticizing the other parent in front of the kids and reducing some of the snarks and jabs that happen in your communications with the other parent. These remarks can make you feel good, perhaps, at that moment, but they don't help the overall relationship with the other parent.

Even though the relationship between the parties has changed, the fact that they are parents to their children will not change. When spouses do not have children, they can often truly go their separate ways after a divorce, but for parents, a true parting of the ways isn't possible. Being parents means that despite their negative feelings for one another, these two people will be involved in each other's lives for the rest of their lives, at least as far as their children are concerned. There will be recitals to attend, games to watch, graduations to attend, weddings, and maybe even grandchildren one day. The goal is to get the parents to a place where they can attend these types of events without setting the child up for uncomfortable interactions with their parents where they don't really know where to sit or whom to talk to.

Parents going through a separation are expected to manage their own emotions while also continuing to parent their children. Be kind to yourself. You do not have to be perfect. Having a strong support system can help. Before things get out of control, seek help for yourself, whether it be professional help in the form of therapy or support from your community. You may need to lean on your friends and family members, and that's OK. Some churches even offer support groups for people going through a divorce. Seek out the resources you need, because when you are a parent, you don't have the luxury of checking out while you manage your emotions.

Evidence in Child Custody Cases

In general, parties can request evidence that is relevant to the pending subject matter or is likely to lead to the discovery of admissible evidence.[18] In custody cases, we request evidence related to the health and welfare of the minor children, such as the children's medical records, their school records, communications between the parents and between the parents and children, as well as any communications between the parents and any third parties about the children, the other party, or the lawsuit itself. The most common categories of evidence used in custody cases are:

- Children's school and medical records
- Emails
- Text messages
- Social media postings
- Electronic devices such as computers, phones, and/or tablets
- Photographs
- Audio recordings
- Videos
- Private investigator reports

Evidence in custody cases is usually obtained in one of three ways: through a request for production of documents, through the service of subpoenas, or by taking the deposition of the opposing party. If the information is in the possession of a third party, and I don't want to rely upon the opposing party to produce the evidence, then I will often serve a subpoena on the third party asking that they produce the information. Discovery requests to the opposing party can take a long time. The opposing party can take up to sixty days to answer the request for production of documents.

If timing is an issue, serving a subpoena may be the better route to go unless the information you need is in the possession of the opposing party. If that's the case, your lawyer might want to consider taking the deposition of the opposing party. Your lawyer can serve a request for production of documents along with the notice of deposition that requires the other party to produce their documents at the deposition. Only twenty-five days' notice is needed in North Carolina to take the other party's deposition if you have also requested that they produce documents at their deposition.[19] The downside to this approach, however, is that depositions can be expensive.

A party has a duty to preserve evidence when the party has notice that the evidence is relevant to the litigation or when the party should know that the evidence may be relevant to future litigation.

How can I get medical and mental health records?

In most custody cases, typically if there are mental health records, one side or the other will argue that those records are relevant to the custody action. If you want to request the other side's mental health records, you will need to do so through a judge-signed subpoena. Alternatively, if both sides have mental health records that need to be produced, each party may be willing to sign a release so that the records can be produced.

Can I delete evidence that might be harmful to my case?

Deleting evidence is a big no-no. A party has a duty to preserve evidence when the party has notice that the evidence is relevant to the litigation or when the party should know that the evidence may be relevant to future litigation. Practically speaking, what this means is that if you think you could be involved in a custody lawsuit, you should not delete your text messages, your emails, or your Facebook or other social media posts. If you delete evidence, you run the risk that the court can draw an inference against you that the deleted evidence would have been adverse to your interests.

For example, if you and your partner get separated, there is a chance that a custody lawsuit might be filed. At that point, you are under a duty to preserve evidence, and if you choose to consult with a lawyer, the lawyer should advise you of your duty to preserve evidence. In addition to not deleting evidence, preserving evidence might include making a backup of evidence that could be destroyed. For example, the data on cell phones can be easily destroyed, so you may need to consider making a back-up of your cell phone.

How do you obtain evidence from electronic devices?

In most cases, in order to obtain evidence from electronic devices, you will need to hire an expert. Most lawyers are not skilled at duplicating the stored data on a cell phone, and even if they are, you will need to hire a digital forensic expert who can not only make an exact copy of the computer hard drive, the tablet, or the cell phone data, but also testify for you in court. Once the data on the device has been duplicated, whether or not you can view the information on the duplicate image may be up to the court to decide, but assuming that the parties have agreed that each of their devices can be copied, the lawyers typically provide a list of search terms that are "off limits" to the other side. For example, if my client's device was being copied, I would request that any communications to or from me be filtered out and not provided to the other side, so I would have the opportunity to review that information before anything that is potentially privileged is sent to the other side.

What kind of evidence do you generally obtain through private investigators?

In custody cases, a private investigator can be useful to obtain evidence of the other party engaging in behavior that would not be in in the best interest of the children. For example, if you suspect the other party is engaging in drug use, frequenting bars, or driving without a license or while under the influence of alcohol, a private investigator might be of assistance to help you gather the evidence you need to prove these allegations.

Substance Abuse Issues in Child Custody Cases

The "Substance Abuse" section is based on season 1, episode 14, of the podcast with my law partner Carrie Tortora.

Some of the most emotionally charged decisions separating parents must make are those surrounding child custody. Determining the optimal custodial arrangement for the children takes many factors into consideration, including the ages of the children, the work and travel schedules of the parents, and so on. When one parent is abusing drugs or alcohol, these highly emotional decisions become even more complex. While the best interests of the children always come first in custody decisions, ensuring the safety and stability of the children is paramount when substance abuse is involved.

Substance abuse refers to the overindulgence or dependence on alcohol and/or drugs, including the overuse of prescription drugs. The *Journal of Studies on Alcohol and Drugs* reported a link between alcohol use and divorce,[20] finding that an increase in alcohol consumption increases the divorce rate and that an increase in the divorce rate brings about an increase in alcohol consumption. If you or your ex-spouse has a substance abuse problem, this section will help explain how substance abuse can affect a custody case in North Carolina and will offer suggestions to assist you in making child custody decisions that are in the best interests of your children.

How might substance abuse impact my child custody case?

Although in recent decades, it has become less common for judges to award full or primary physical custody to one parent over the other, when evidence of substance abuse exists, a judge may be more likely to award custody to the parent without the substance abuse problem. In addition, the court may order supervised visitation between the children and the parent with a recent history of drug or alcohol abuse in certain cases. Supervision may be provided by a close friend or family member that

> **While the best interests of the children always come first in custody decisions, ensuring the safety and stability of the children is paramount when substance abuse is involved.**

both parents have agreed upon, or by a paid supervisor. For example, some child psychologists provide this service. In Wake County, Time Together[21] offers a safe, drop-off environment for supervised visitations, and All Kids First[22] arranges for professional supervision in public locations such as parks, restaurants, and museums.

When cases are settled out of court, you can negotiate for different parameters and terms in the agreement that address concerns you may have about substance abuse. For example, the agreement might state that neither parent should consume alcohol while the children are in his or her care. You can get as specific as you'd like in the separation agreement, and the agreement could require that any positive drug test will equate to suspended visitation for a period of time.

What evidence is needed to prove substance abuse?

Evidence such as a DUI, sporadic employment history, or hospitalization for drug- or alcohol-related

If you have reason to believe that the other party is using alcohol or drugs, you can file a motion with the court requesting that the court require the other party submit to a drug test or alcohol screening.

issues can be used to help prove substance abuse in your child custody case. If you have reason to believe that the other party is using alcohol or drugs, you can file a motion with the court requesting that the court require the other party submit to a drug test or alcohol screening. Alcohol/drug screening options include:

- Periodic alcohol monitoring, which involves either the installation of a device on the parent's vehicle or a portable breathalyzer
- Continuous alcohol monitoring bracelets
- Periodic or random drug testing (a multi-panel hair follicle drug test is preferred), which typically coincides with the custodial period

Your child's other parent may be hesitant to agree to take a drug test due to the cost involved. If that is the case, you may wish to include a clause in the separation agreement or custody order stating that the parent requesting the drug/alcohol test will pay for the test unless the test results are positive. The separation agreement can also shift the burden for requesting drug or alcohol tests to a third party, such as a counselor, who will meet with the parent and make recommendations on the frequency and timing of the drug/alcohol tests.

If I suspect my ex-spouse is abusing drugs or alcohol when I drop off the children with them, what are my rights?

If a court order is in place that outlines custody arrangements and you refuse to honor the custody arrangement due to suspected alcohol or drug abuse, there is a risk the other side will seek to hold you in contempt. However, in these situations, use your best judgment as a parent. If you have good reason to withhold the visit out of a legitimate concern for your children's safety, the court is less likely to hold you in contempt. With that said, if you have doubts about whether you may be overreacting, consult with a lawyer, a therapist, or other professional with an objective opinion on the facts of your case before taking action.

What if I am the parent with the substance abuse problem, or what if I am being accused of having a problem?

First, if you find yourself turning to drugs or alcohol, get the help you need. Depending upon the situation, treatment may involve counseling, Alcoholics Anonymous, or rehabilitation (whether inpatient or outpatient). While seeking treatment may temporarily affect your custody arrangements—for example, your custodial time might be supervised until you can prove that you are sober and/or clean for a given length of time—recognize that this temporary solution allows you to preserve your relationship with your children, while allowing you the time to get the help that you need. The beauty of child custody is it is not set in stone. Even if you have a court order, in North Carolina, custody schedules are modifiable until your children turn eighteen.

If you believe that you do not have a problem and that your child's other parent is making false accusations in order to gain an advantage in the custody case, it may be time to take proactive steps to combat their accusations. For example, you might quit drinking altogether, and/or agree to wear a continuous monitoring bracelet in order to prove that you are alcohol-free.

The needs and best interests of the children should always come first in a child custody case. Knowing your rights will help you protect your children while also preserving their relationships with both parents and, most importantly, will help ensure a safe and stable environment during this potentially tumultuous time.

Relocation Issues

In today's society, relocation is becoming more common; however, if you have children and are separated from your children's other parent, relocation can present a different set of challenges. Following a divorce, a parent may obtain employment in a different state or remarry and, as a result, wish to move to another state. While a court cannot prevent a parent from moving out of state, the court can order that the children remain in North Carolina with the other parent.

It is well established in North Carolina that when a trial court is deciding whether to allow a parent to move from the state with the minor children, the best interest and welfare of the children is the most important issue. Before deciding whether a relocation is in the best interest of a child, the court will consider several factors.

While a court cannot prevent a parent from moving out of state, the court can order that the children remain in North Carolina with the other parent.

First, the court will determine the advantages of the relocation in terms of whether the move will improve the life of the child. In making this determination, the court will take into account how well established the child is in North Carolina, such as how long the child has been in school here, whether the child has extended family in North Carolina, and whether the child has any special needs that may cause them to have difficulties creating new relationships in a new environment if the relocation is allowed.

The court will also consider the motives of the custodial parent in desiring to move and the likelihood that the moving parent will continue to promote the children's relationship with the other parent after the move. In addition, the court will take into account the reasons why the other parent objects to the move and whether a realistic visitation schedule can be arranged that will preserve and continue to foster the children's relationship with the non-moving parent.

When parents live in different states, it is not uncommon for the custody schedule to provide that the child will live with one parent during the majority of the school year and with the other parent during the summer and other school breaks. In addition, the schedule may also provide that the parent who lives out of state may visit with the child in North Carolina at least once per month.

Due to advances in technology, such as FaceTime and Skype, the distance created by a move is not the prohibitive factor it once was when determining whether to permit relocation; however, every situation is unique. If you are considering a move that will affect your current custody schedule, or if your ex-spouse is considering a move that you oppose, you should consult with an attorney who can help you evaluate whether the court would consider the move to be in the best interest of your children.

Third-Party Custody

The thought of having to leave your child with a third-party caregiver for an extended period of time is not something anyone wants to consider; however, circumstances can arise in which acting in the best interest of the child requires parents to temporarily relinquish custody to a third party. If a parent is ill or otherwise incapacitated for a temporary period of time, they may need the help of a friend or family member to care for their child. Before making the decision to entrust your child to a third party in a time of need, there are several steps you should take to ensure that your child will be returned to you when you get back on your feet.

The United States Constitution protects the fundamental right of parents to make decisions concerning the care, custody, and control of their children; however, if a legal parent, whether biological or adoptive, acts in a manner that is inconsistent with their constitutionally protected status, the parent may lose this protected status and might find themselves in a custody dispute with a nonparent, like a third-party caregiver. Whether a parent has acted in a manner inconsistent with his or her constitutionally protected status must be made on a case-by-case basis. The parent's conduct and intent are relevant in making this determination.

In such cases, the court would consider the reason for the relinquishment of custody. Was the parent suffering from poor health? Were they required to serve in the military? Were they unemployed and trying to find work? First and foremost, the parent needs to inform the caregiver that the relinquishment of custody is temporary and that the parent fully intends to resume custody once they are back on their feet. Second, the parent needs to maintain consistent contact with their children. While in-person visits are preferable, if such visits are not possible, then daily telephone or other electronic contact with the children should be made. The parent should also continue to provide financial support for the children to the extent that they are able. One option is to set up a custodial bank account for the child with the parent and third-party caregiver as custodians. In addition, the parent should ask the caregiver to keep them informed with respect to the child's daily activities, including any medical or dental appointments, extracurricular activities, and school functions, and the parent should attend these activities as much as possible.

If you are considering allowing someone else to care for your child for an extended period of time, it is important to consult with a professional who is skilled in this area to help guide you through the process.

Grandparent Visitation

 The "Grandparent Visitation" section is based on season 1, episode 8, of the podcast with my law partner Stephanie Gibbs.

When a couple separates, we normally think about a custody schedule being put in place that sets forth when the children will spend time with each of their parents, but in some cases, grandparents might also have a right to visitation. Grandparents can seek visitation with a grandchild pursuant to N.C. Gen. Stat. § 50-13.2(b1), which provides that an order for child custody may include visitation rights for any grandparent of the child as the court, in its discretion, deems appropriate. However, in order for a grandparent to seek visitation, there must be an ongoing parental custody dispute, and the child's family must not be an intact family.[23] In North Carolina, an intact family is not limited to situations where both biological parents live together. An intact family can include a single parent living with his or her child,[24] as well as a married natural parent, stepparent, and a child living in a single residence.[25]

> **Grandparents can seek visitation with a grandchild pursuant to N.C. Gen. Stat. § 50-13.2(b1), which provides that an order for child custody may include visitation rights for any grandparent of the child as the court, in its discretion, deems appropriate.**

Grandparents might want to seek visitation with their grandchildren if they have a strained relationship with one or both of the grandchildren's parents who will not allow the grandparents to see the children. It can be one or both parents who the grandparents fear will not allow visitation, and the grandparents want to ensure that they are able to see the grandchildren moving forward before a permanent custody order is entered. Alternatively, an adult child may have a grave illness, such as cancer, and the grandparents are uncertain whether the other parent, who is the soon to be the ex-spouse, will allow the grandparents to see the children if the sick parent goes into the hospital, dies, or is otherwise unable to exercise custody with the children. Another reason grandparents may wish to seek visitation with grandchildren is if the grandparents fear that their adult child will move away or remarry or otherwise end up in a situation that would make visitation with the children difficult or impossible.

How does the process work?

If there is an ongoing custody dispute between the children's parents, the first thing the grandparents should do is file a motion to intervene asking the court to allow them to become a party to the case. Attached to your motion would be something called an intervenor's complaint, and in both of these documents you would have to allege that certain circumstances exist that would persuade the court you should first be allowed into the case as a party, and second that you should be granted visitation with the grandchildren because it's in the best interest of the children that you and those grandchildren preserve your relationship.

Grandparents seeking visitation with their grandchildren should state to the court that they have a substantial relationship with the children; that they are the grandparents of the children; how long they have known the children; how they've cared for the children; and what they have done for the children physically, emotionally, and financially. Once these facts have been presented to the court, the court will decide whether the grandparents are allowed to come into the case as a party, and if they are allowed, they will have a table in the courtroom just like the parents and their lawyers, and they will be able to offer evidence as to why they should be allowed to visit with their grandchildren and why it's in the grandchildren's best interest that visitation be ordered.

Do the parents have any defenses to a motion to intervene?

Parents can object to a motion to intervene filed by their children's grandparents. First, the motion must be timely filed such that it does not prejudice the other parties. If grandparents try to file their motion to get into the case after the depositions have been done and discovery has been completed and after the time has passed for the parents to investigate the merits of the grandparents' claim, a judge may say that the motion to intervene was not timely filed. If the grandparents wait too long, their delay is potentially prejudicial to the children's parents, because at that point the parents would not have a chance to gather the evidence they need to defend their positions. Accordingly, the judge may deny the motion to intervene, and therefore, the grandparents are not allowed into the case and cannot ask for visitation until some later date.

It is important to remember that there is a very narrow window of opportunity for a grandparent to seek visitation. Once a permanent custody order has been entered, grandparents no longer have an opportunity to seek visitation with the children unless a motion to modify custody is filed at some point in the future by one of the parents. Grandparents may get a second bite of the apple since custody orders are modifiable in North Carolina (meaning they can be changed) until the child turns eighteen. If a custody order gets entered when a child is very young, there is a likelihood at some point one of the parents will file a motion and ask the court to change that order. With that

At a very basic level, the intact family rule is a protection of a parent's constitutional right to the care, custody, and control of their child.

said, it is still better for grandparents to file their motion to intervene in the first instance rather than waiting for a modification, because there is a chance that a modification may never happen, and even if it does, it may not happen until many years have passed since the grandparents have seen the children.

Another defense parents may have to an intervention by their children's grandparents is the intact family rule. As stated above, in order for grandparents to seek visitation, there must be an ongoing parental custody dispute, and the children's family must not be an intact family. At a very basic level, the intact family rule is a protection of a parent's constitutional right to the care, custody, and control of their child. In other words, a grandparent can't demand visitation where there is no strain on the family, such as a divorce or a stepparent adoption, and no one is seeking a new custody arrangement. If the intact family is just living its life, a grandparent can't try to barge into that life and demand to visit with the children. In those cases, whether or not the children will be allowed to visit with the grandparents is completely up to the parents.

In defense to a motion to intervene, the parents can also argue that allowing the grandparents to intervene is not in the best interest of the child because the child should not be exposed to the grandparents' lifestyle, habits, or conditions. For example, if the grandparent smokes, abuses substances, has a criminal history, or otherwise engages in behavior such that the grandparent would not be a good influence upon the child, it may not be in the child's best interest to have visitation with the grandparent. The burden is on the grandparent to prove that visitation with the grandparent would be in the child's best interest. In cases where the grandparent and the child's parents have such a poor relationship that the stressful interactions between the parents and the grandparent would have a negative effect upon the child, visitation with the grandparent may not be in the child's best interest.

What does grandparent visitation look like?

If a grandparent is successful and the court awards the grandparent visitation with his or her grandchild, the visitation time will be independent of either of the parents. Essentially, the court will carve out time during the month, generally on a routine and regular basis, that the child will spend time with the grandparent. Often, this time will be a set day or two a month, a week or two in the summer, and perhaps some time over Christmas, the child's birthday, or other holiday time. The grandparent's time with the child will be included in the custody order along with the regular schedule allocated to the child's parents, and the schedule will reflect the grandparent's day or days and holiday and summertime. If for some reason the child's parents do not allow the grandparent the time with the child as set forth in the order, the grandparent can seek the assistance of the court in enforcing the order.

A parenting coordinator (PC) is defined by N.C. Gen. Stat. § 50-90 as a neutral person who meets the qualifications under the statute to help parents work out high-conflict child custody issues.

CHAPTER 4

Parenting Coordinators

 This chapter is based on season 1, episode 5, of the podcast with family law attorney and parenting coordinator Katie King.

If you are involved in a high-conflict custody case, you may be able to ask the court to appoint a parenting coordinator in your case. A parenting coordinator (PC) is defined by N.C. Gen. Stat. § 50-90 as a neutral person who meets the qualifications under the statute to help parents work out high-conflict child custody issues. A PC has to be a lawyer or someone with a degree in psychology, social work, counseling, or other related field. A PC must also take twenty-four hours of training related to developmental stages of children, dynamics of high-conflict families, the stages and effects of divorce, problem-solving techniques, mediation, and legal issues.[26] With this special training, a PC can be appointed to help high-conflict families address their custody issues and keep the parents from going to court all of the time by helping manage the day to-day logistics of a custody schedule that the court just doesn't have the resources to address.

When a PC is appointed, the judge will issue a PC appointment order that will set forth anything that the judge wants the PC to decide. In Wake County, a checkbox form order includes various areas over which the PC can be given authority. Among other things, the PC can be given the authority to address health-care decisions, issues related to transportation and exchanges, appearance or grooming issues, extracurricular activities, or participation in visitation by significant others. The judge can also appoint a PC to deal with specific issues that aren't included in the checkboxes. For example, if the parents have a decision coming up with respect to school selection, the judge could allow the PC to make that decision.

The PC's authority to make a decision comes from the PC appointment order. If the order does not specify that the PC has the authority to make a decision about a certain issue, then the PC is unable to do so. For example, if a family has an issue relating to holiday time with the children, but the PC appointment order does not include the sharing of holiday time as an area of authority for the PC, even if there is a legitimate dispute about the holidays, the PC cannot make the decision about that issue. In addition, PCs are not able to address financial issues, which can be difficult for the parties to understand since there is

The job of the PC is to help the family implement their custody order and to fill in gaps where something isn't specifically set forth in the custody order.

so much potential crossover between custody issues and their financial impact on the parties. For example, if the PC is asked to make a decision about extracurricular activities or private school, the decision is likely to have a financial impact; however, the PC is unable to do anything about that financial impact on the parties.

PCs are also unable to change the parties' custody order in a significant way. The job of the PC is to help the family implement their custody order and to fill in gaps where something isn't specifically set forth in the custody order. The PC may not be able to change the parties' schedule, but the PC can tweak the schedule if need be. For example, dad is flying internationally and, because of the cost of plane tickets, needs to arrive back in town at 8:00 p.m., but the order says he is supposed to exchange the children with mom at 6:00 p.m. In that case, the PC could decide that the parties will exchange the children at 8:00 p.m. on this one occasion. This is an example of a PC making a decision that does not significantly alter the custody order, and the PC has the authority to make these little changes that don't affect the basic timesharing arrangement. On the other hand, there may be times when the parties' custody order is silent on a particular issue. Perhaps the order contains a holiday schedule, but the schedule doesn't include Halloween. If Halloween becomes an issue, the PC can't go back and create a Halloween schedule where one did not exist in the first place.

Lawyers versus Therapists

Whether to have a lawyer or therapist appointed as the PC really depends on the specific family and what the family needs. As an attorney representing my client who may need a PC, in most cases, I will typically want a lawyer to serve as the PC; however, that's not to say there aren't excellent mental-health professionals who serve as PCs. They could be a good fit for families where the parties or children have significant mental-health issues or some other reason that a mental-health professional needs to be involved.

A lot of times when helping select a PC for my clients, I am looking for a PC who I think has a particular qualification for the particular family, not just in the context of mental-health professional versus lawyer, but maybe whether the PC has children of similar ages to those of the family who need the PC. The idea is to find a PC with whom the family will connect. Having a PC can be uncomfortable for families, and it is helpful to have a PC who can establish a positive connection from the outset. At one point or another, one or both of the parents will disagree with whatever decision the PC makes. If the parents can at least connect with the PC on a basic personal level, it can help them live with what might otherwise be a more difficult PC decision.

In many situations, having a PC involved in your case is like having a third parent in the situation; thus, it is important for the families to trust that the PC is going to give them practical advice. Odds are good, however, that one parent or the other is not going to like the decision that the PC makes. In those cases, if the parties continuously agree that they don't like what the PC is doing, the better option is that you make decisions for your family yourself as the parents and not have a PC make those decisions. A positive consequence of the PC process is that sometimes the parents dislike the decisions of the PC so much and dislike allocating their authority to a third party that they begin to learn how to make parental decisions on their own.

Part of the goal of being a PC is to help families with their communication skills and to equip them with some of the tools they can use to start trying to resolve some of these custodial issues on their own. For example, the PC can help each party learn how to respond to the other party's emails. If one parent sends the other parent an email with more than one idea, question, or discussion point, what is the best way for that parent to respond to the email? The PC may recommend responding point by point. Maybe the points get numbered. Maybe if you have nothing else to add, you just acknowledge that you've received and read the email, and agree to whatever the points are.

How to Have a PC Appointed

If you think you might benefit from having a PC, the first step is to have a custody order or to be involved in the custody litigation process. If you are already involved in the custody litigation process, the judge can appoint a PC at any point in a custody proceeding if they determine that the case is a high-conflict case and the parties have the ability to pay the cost of the PC.[27] The parties may also consent to the appointment of a PC.

If you don't have a custody order but would still like to have a PC, parents can create a private, contractual relationship with a PC. These cases are different than the ones involving court-appointed PCs discussed above because the process is not controlled by statute. In these cases, the PC is essentially functioning as an arbitrator, meaning that the PC would be a decision-maker in the parents' custody conflicts when they can't agree because even in the best custody situations, conflict can arise over school choice or communication or any number of issues related to parenting children.

Cost

When an attorney is acting as a PC, that attorney is most likely going to charge a lower hourly rate than their normal lawyer rate. In addition, in the PC appointment order, the judge will state how the fees are to be divided between the parties. In most cases, the fees for the PC are divided 50/50 between the parties, but if you have a case where one parent makes substantially more money than the other parent, the fees may be allocated between the parties unevenly. The parties might share the PC fee in proportion to their incomes. For example, if one parent earns sixty percent of the family income, and the other parent earns forty percent of the family income, they might proportionally pay their individual share for the PC. That way both parents have some skin in the game, and sharing fees is fair to both of them and not an undue burden on one party or the other. While the process still has a cost associated with it, that cost is usually lower than if both parties have to pay each of their lawyers to bring an issue before the court.

In addition, a parent coordinator has the authority to reallocate the fee if one of the parents is abusing the process. If the same party continually brings frivolous issues to the PC, the PC can allocate one hundred percent of the fees to that party in an attempt to encourage the party to stop abusing the process. Oftentimes, the PC will inform the parties that if a certain issue is raised again, the party bringing the issue to the PC will get a bill for one hundred percent of the fees. Hopefully, it doesn't happen very often, but it is helpful when you have one party abusing the process that there is some relief available for the other parent.

Improving Communication

In most cases where a PC is involved, the parties have difficulty communicating with each other. PCs will often try to create systems so that the parties can learn to communicate more practically and appropriately with one another. Streamlining communication can be a huge issue with high-conflict families. One resource that can help is a program called Our Family Wizard.[28] This online platform creates a forum for the parents that documents when an email was sent and when it was read. It helps do away with the excuse that a parent didn't respond to an email because they didn't receive it. Our Family Wizard also includes a family calendar and allows the parties to give professional access to the PC, so the PC can log into the program and review the parties' communications to make sure the communications are appropriate. Sometimes the parents behave a little bit better if they know their PC is monitoring their emails with the other parent. Our Family Wizard is often a better alternative than having to pay the PC to screen all of each parent's emails before the emails are sent to the other parent. Having the PC screen emails can be cost prohibitive and also doesn't further the goal of teaching the parties how to communicate with one another. Ultimately, the goal of PC work is to help parents avoid court and to equip them with the tools to have a better parenting relationship with the other parent. The role of the PC is to minimize the potential for conflict and, most importantly, to have peace for the children of these families.

Confidentiality

PC families are almost always represented by attorneys, which means they likely have become accustomed to having confidential, privileged communications with their lawyers. The same does not hold true, however, of the communications they have with their PC. Even if the PC happens to be a lawyer, the PC is not the lawyer of either of the parties; thus,

> **Any email you send to the PC or to the other parent is a potential exhibit in your case. So don't send an email that you would be ashamed to read out loud in court one day.**

the parties' communications with the PC are not confidential. Even though the PC may not necessarily forward every email they receive from one parent to the other parent, they can. Likewise, if the attorney for the other parent sends the PC a request for all of the email communications, or if the judge subpoenas the PC's file, all those communications are going to be fair game and subject to being produced to the other side. It is important for PC clients to understand that they should not send any email to the PC that they don't want the other side to see. In addition, PC clients should not send emails to the PC and tell the PC not to share the email with the other side, because even if the PC doesn't intend to share the email, it doesn't prevent the other attorney from requesting the email communications or the judge from issuing a subpoena.

Any email you send to the PC or to the other parent is a potential exhibit in your case. So don't send an email that you would be ashamed to read out loud in court one day. Use good commonsense as a parent. When you are a parent involved in a custody case, everything you do, and everything you say is under scrutiny, which can be stressful, but it is also a good thing to remember when you are communicating with the other parent. The judge is tasked with deciding what is in the best interest of your children, and how you parent your children and communicate with your children's other parent is directly related to that standard. For so long as you have involved yourself willingly or not in this process, you have to deal with it, and you have to learn how to parent while being watched for a certain period of time.

The Process after the PC Has Been Appointed

In most cases, before making a decision, the PC will make sure that the parties have first attempted to work out the issue on their own without involving the PC. The PC should not be used as a way for one party to work around having to communicate with the other party. Once the PC determines there is actually an issue in dispute, the PC will hear from both parents on the issue to determine the position of each. Oftentimes, communication with the PC is via email, which can be both good and bad. Email communications help create transparency because it is clear what the PC has communicated to the parties. Email can be cumbersome, however, depending upon the complexity of the issue that needs to be addressed. In those situations, a phone call or meeting might be warranted.

Once the PC has heard from both parties, the PC may need to talk to third parties. For example, the PC might need to speak with the child's therapist, or depending on the issue, there might be a doctor involved or perhaps the child's teachers. The PC appointment order provides that the parents will sign the releases necessary for the PC to talk to whomever the PC needs to talk to in order to make a decision about the issue at hand. Once the PC has gathered all of the research needed and has made a decision, the PC will typically send the decision to the parents in writing by email. The email will explain what the decision is along with the reasoning behind it. In most cases, the email will be sent to the parents and their lawyers. The PC statute and the PC appointment order tell the parents that the decision of a PC is binding on them just like an order of the court, so they will need to comply with that decision unless the judge reviews it and says otherwise. If a PC makes a decision that one of the parties thinks is incorrect or that the PC did not have the authority to make, that party can file a request with the court for the judge to review the decision. If the judge determines that the PC should not have made the decision, the judge has the authority to overrule the PC decision.

What happens if one parent does not follow the decision of the PC?

If one parent does not follow the PC's decision, the other parent can file a motion and ask that the parent not following the decision be held in contempt. In

> **If the case is so high conflict that the parties cannot utilize the PC in an effective way to help them make decisions together, it may be better if one parent has the authority to make the final decision.**

addition, in some cases, the PC has the ability to file a report to the court if the PC believes that the existing custody order is no longer in the best interest of the children or if the PC is not qualified to address or resolve certain issues in the case.[29] As a result of that report to the court, if the judge finds that one of the parties is not complying with the order, the judge might issue a show cause order to determine whether the party should be held in contempt. In cases where a PC is involved, the parties often feel like it is the job of the PC to police the custody order; however, the PC can only remind parents what their obligations are pursuant to the custody order and clarify them where necessary.

Are there times when having a parent coordinator is not helpful?

When you have two parents who need some help with decision-making, a PC can be a really good thing in the right case. In other cases, however, some parents will overuse the PC in an attempt to perpetuate their own position in the case. They will try to use the PC to work around the other parent and to avoid co-parenting. In these cases, rather than have a PC, it may be that the parties should not share legal custody and decision-making authority with respect to the child. If the case is so high conflict that the parties cannot utilize the PC in an effective way to help them make decisions together, it may be better if one parent has the authority to make the final decision. In some cases, the amount of time that it takes for two parents to attempt to reach a decision about anything can be detrimental to the child. Nothing ever gets done. The child never gets to play soccer or basketball or go to whatever extracurricular activity they want to attend because if one parent suggests it, the other parent is always going to say no or vice versa. If a PC is involved in these types of cases, one parent may continually bring issues to the PC and then most likely will not like the PC decision, so they will ask the court to review the decision. If the PC has to decide every single issue for a family, a lot of families simply can't afford that level of interaction, and it becomes cost prohibitive.

In North Carolina, parents have a legal duty to financially support their children until they reach eighteen years of age and have graduated from high school.

CHAPTER 5

Child Support

In North Carolina, parents have a legal duty to financially support their children until they reach eighteen years of age and have graduated from high school. In most cases, the amount of child support a parent is obligated to pay is calculated pursuant to the North Carolina child support guidelines. The guidelines apply to cases where the parents' combined gross income is $360,000 or less per year and take into account the proportion each parent's income contributes toward the total income of the parties. Gross income includes but is not limited to salaries, wages, commissions, bonuses, dividends, severance pay, income from rental properties, social security benefits, workers compensation, and disability payments.

The amount of child support each parent owes depends upon several factors, including the number of

If the combined gross income of the parents exceeds $360,000 per year, rather than using the child support guidelines, evidence of the child's actual expenses will be used to determine the appropriate amount of child support.

nights the child spends at each parent's residence, the cost of the child's health insurance, any work-related childcare expenses, and any extraordinary child-related expenses. Extraordinary expenses include such things as special or private education to meet a child's particular educational needs, as well as expenses incurred for transporting the child between the parents' houses.

When child support is calculated pursuant to the North Carolina child support guidelines, one of three worksheets will be used: A, B, or C. Worksheet A applies when one parent has primary custody, worksheet B applies when the parents share custody, and worksheet C applies when one parent has primary custody of at least one of the children and the other parent has primary custody of the other children.

For example, if the parties have 50/50 custody of their two children, we will use worksheet B to calculate child support. If we assume mom and dad each make $5,000 per month, and mom pays $200 per month for the children's health insurance, as well as $1,000 per month for work-related childcare expenses, using the child support guidelines, dad would owe mom $600 per month as child support. If you would like to calculate your own child support scenarios, the child support guidelines and worksheets can be found online at https://ncchildsupport.com/ecoa/cseGuideLines.htm.

In certain circumstances, however, the child support guidelines do not apply. In those cases, child support will be calculated based upon the needs of the child and the ability of the parents to pay support. One circumstance in which the guidelines do not apply involves cases in which the parents have a high combined income. If the combined gross income of the parents exceeds $360,000 per year, rather than using the child support guidelines, evidence of the child's actual expenses will be used to determine the appropriate amount of child support.

Another circumstance in which the guidelines may not apply is if either party requests a deviation from the guidelines. A deviation may be requested if application of the guidelines would be unjust or inappropriate. For example, if the guideline amount of child support would exceed or not meet the reasonable needs of the child, a parent may request a deviation from the child support guidelines.

Paying for College

In North Carolina, a parent's obligation to pay support for his or her children ends when the child turns eighteen and has graduated from high school. There is no requirement that either parent pay for the child's college education, and a court cannot require that the parents pay for their children's college education. In some cases, however, parties agree in a private contract how they will fund their children's college education. The parents will agree to divide the expenses in some manner, or one parent will agree to pay for all of the children's college expenses. Typically, if one parent agrees to pay for all of the college expenses, it is in exchange for paying less of some other obligation such as alimony.

If you are considering adding provisions for the payment of college expenses to your separation agreement or other contract, it is important to also consider adding limitations with respect to how much will be paid and for how long. For example, how many semesters of college are you willing to pay for? What if your child decides to take a year off from school and then resume classes? Are you still responsible? Does your requirement to pay include both public and private colleges? A sample college expense provision may look something like this one:

> College Expenses. Provided that the child begins college by age twenty (20), the parties agree that they shall equally pay, with Husband being responsible for fifty percent (50%) and Wife being responsible for fifty percent (50%) of all college expenses for the child related to the costs of tuition, books, fees, and room and board for eight (8) semesters, or until age twenty-five (25) unless the parties agree otherwise, at a rate not higher than the then cost of an in-state tuition and room and board rate at the University of North Carolina at Chapel Hill. The costs of each parent shall

be reduced by the financial aid or scholarships received by the child. Payments shall be paid directly to the child's college or university unless the parties agree otherwise.

Changing Your Child Support Obligation

Child support ordered by a court may be reduced or increased if there has been a "substantial change of circumstances" since the court established the amount due. The "substantial change" might be an increase in the cost of the child's needs. For example, the cost of the child's health insurance could double, or the child might need braces or counseling. Alternatively, the "substantial change" could be a change in one or both parents' ability to pay the amount of support previously ordered. Under North Carolina law, in a proceeding to modify child support, payable pursuant to an order that is at least three years old, if there is a difference of at least 15 percent between the amount of child support payable under the old order versus what would be owed by calculating child support using the parties' current incomes and circumstances, it presumptively qualifies as a substantial change. A judge will first determine whether there has been a substantial change that merits an increase or decrease before deciding whether to alter the existing amount of child support due.

If parents have agreed upon an amount of child support in a separation agreement or other contract, the amount may be modified by amendment of the

Child support ordered by a court may be reduced or increased if there has been a "substantial change of circumstances" since the court established the amount due.

contract. If the parents are unable to agree on a new amount, one or both parents may file a lawsuit to establish the amount of child support. In this situation, a judge must initially presume that the amount the parents agreed upon in their contract is reasonable. The parent wishing to change the amount must overcome that legal presumption.

When a Parent Fails to Pay Child Support

If the support is court ordered, the parent not receiving support may file a contempt motion in which they ask the court to enforce the support order by holding the non-paying parent in contempt. A parent held in contempt faces a number of penalties, including possible jail time and/or the payment of the other party's attorney fees. If the child support is due pursuant to the terms of a separation agreement or other contract, the parent who is supposed to receive the child support payments may file a lawsuit for breach of contract and specific performance in order to enforce the provisions of the contract. Alternatively, depending upon the circumstances, the party may elect to file a lawsuit and ask the court to establish child support. In such cases, the child support provisions contained in the separation agreement will most likely be given a presumption of reasonableness, which will need to be rebutted in order to change the amount of child support that is being paid.[30]

Given the complexity of these issues, if you are involved in a case in which child support is to be determined, you should consider consulting with a family law attorney since the amount of child support may vary depending upon a number of circumstances.

Equitable distribution, is the distribution of property between separated spouses.

CHAPTER 6 ■

Equitable
Distribution

North Carolina General Statutes (NCGS) § 50-20 through § 50-22 address equitable distribution, which is the distribution of property between separated spouses. Marital property is any property acquired by the spouses during their marriage and prior to their date of separation and presently owned by either spouse on the date of separation, except for property that was received by one of the spouses as an inheritance or a gift from a third party. Marital property can include but is not limited to real estate, cars, household goods and furnishings, financial accounts, pension and retirement accounts, stock options, and even frequent flier miles, credit card points, and pets. Gifts between spouses are also marital property unless a contrary intention is expressed in the conveyance. Marital debt is also part of the equation and can be divided between the parties. A claim for equitable distribution must be at least pending with the court when the divorce judgment is entered, or you will lose your right to bring a claim for equitable distribution.[31]

Identifying the Property

The first step the court must take in an equitable distribution action is to identify all of the property. While this concept may seem very basic, it is important to note that not everything will constitute "property." North Carolina does not define the concept of property in its equitable distribution statute, and cases addressing the issue have not offered a specific definition. Whether something is considered "property" will vary "according to the subject treated of and according to the context."[32] In other words, because the definition of property is so broad, whether something constitutes property will be determined on a case-by-case basis. Practically speaking, most items in equitable distribution cases do constitute property that can later be classified as marital, separate, or divisible.

With that said, a few things have been held not to be property in the context of an equitable distribution case. They are as follows:

- Timber contracts[33]
- VA loan eligibility[34]
- Educational degrees[35]
- Some contingent contractual rights[36]

Classifying the Property:
Presumptions and Burdens of Proof

Property acquired during the marriage is presumed
to be marital unless proven otherwise. As the initial
step in any equitable distribution action, the trial
court will classify all property owned by the parties as
marital or separate as defined by state statute[37] and
"depending upon the proof presented to the trial court
of the nature" of the assets. The burden of showing
the property to be marital is on the party seeking to
classify the asset as marital, and the burden of showing
the property to be separate is on the party seeking to
classify the asset as separate.[38]

Marital property includes "all real and personal
property acquired by either spouse or both spouses
during the course of the marriage and before the date
of the separation of the parties."[39] Separate property is
defined as all real and personal property acquired by
a spouse before marriage or acquired by a spouse by
bequest, devise, descent, or gift during the course of the
marriage. Property acquired in exchange for separate
property shall remain separate property regardless of
whether the title is in the name of the husband or wife
or both and shall not be considered marital property
unless a contrary intention is expressly stated in
the conveyance.[40]

The party who claims the property is marital must
show by the preponderance of the evidence that the
property was "acquired by either spouse or both
spouses during the course of the marriage and before

Property also may be classified as part separate and part marital; such property is considered "dual" in nature.

the date of separation of the parties and is presently owned."[41]

The party seeking to prove the separate nature of property must show by the preponderance of the evidence that the property was "acquired by a spouse by bequest, devise, descent, or gift during the course of the marriage; was acquired by gift from the other spouse during the course of marriage where such an intention is stated in the conveyance; or was acquired in exchange for separate property unless a contrary intention is expressly stated in the conveyance." If one party can prove that property was acquired during the marriage and presently owned on the date of separation, but the other party can also prove that the property was an inheritance or gift, then the property will be considered separate property.[42]

Property also may be classified as part separate and part marital; such property is considered "dual" in nature.[43] Where property is dual in nature, the trial court applies a "source of funds" approach to distinguish between marital and separate contributions to the property.[44] Under this approach, "when both the marital and separate estates contribute assets toward the acquisition of property, each estate is entitled to an interest in the property in the ratio its contribution bears to the total investment in the property."[45]

A party's contribution to dual-natured property need not be monetary. For instance, labor provided in making improvements or repairs to property may result in a portion of the property being classified as marital.[46] Following classification, property classified as marital is distributed by the trial court, while separate property remains unaffected.[47]

With respect to divisible property, the statute creates a presumption that any increase or decrease in the value of marital property after the date of separation and before the date of distribution is divisible property.[48] Thus, a party seeking to have property classified as divisible has to prove that marital property increased or decreased in value and the amount of the change. Once the amount of the increase or decrease has been established, the entire change in value is subject to distribution as divisible property unless the other party proves that the change in value was the result of active efforts by one of the spouses.[49]

NCGS § 50-20 provides for three other categories of divisible property as follows:

1. All property, property rights, or any portion thereof received after the date of separation but before the date of distribution that was acquired as a result of the efforts of either spouse during the marriage and before the date of separation, including, but not limited to, commissions, bonuses, and contractual rights.

2. Passive income from marital property received after the date of separation, including, but not limited to, interest and dividends.

3. Passive increases and passive decreases in marital debt and financing charges and interest related to marital debt.[50]

With respect to these three additional categories, there is not a presumption relating to the classification of these categories as divisible property.[51] The Court of Appeals has stated that the party requesting that property be classified as divisible has the burden of proving "that it is so."[52] As a result, the party seeking to have these types of divisible property distributed by the court has the burden of proving that the property falls within one of the three statutory definitions referenced above without the assistance of a presumption.

Valuation: Time to Call in the Experts

In order for the court to be able to distribute the marital and divisible property, the value of the property must be established. The party seeking to have property classified as marital also has the burden of proving the value of the asset at the date of separation. The trial court does not have an affirmative obligation to value the property if credible evidence is not presented by the parties as to the value of the asset.[53]

Account statements can be used to establish the value of most bank, brokerage, and retirement accounts; however, some assets will require appraisals or valuations performed by an expert. Expert witnesses can be crucial in equitable distribution cases. Some experts you might consider to assist you with your case include real estate appraisers, business valuators, personal property appraisers, or accountants to perform valuations of a pension or stock options or to assist with tracing issues.

Deciding when to hire an expert may depend upon your ability to pay the expert for their services. While real estate appraisals may only cost a few hundred dollars, business valuations often start at $10,000 and go up from there. If you are the business owner, you may think you are in the best position to attest to the value of your business and that your testimony will be sufficient to prove the value of the business to the court. This course of action can be risky if the other side obtains a business valuation and you do not.

The safest course of action is to obtain the valuation up front and not to put yourself in the position of having to rely upon a rebuttal expert to refute the value established by the opposing party.

The safest course of action is to obtain the valuation up front and not to put yourself in the position of having to rely upon a rebuttal expert to refute the value established by the opposing party. If cost is an issue, asking the other side to agree to a joint valuation is a possibility. You can also ask the court for an interim distribution (discussed in more detail later on in this chapter) to help you defray the cost of your expert witnesses.

If you have a real estate appraisal performed in your equitable distribution action, your lawyer will want to make sure that the appraiser is aware that the property must be appraised as of your date of separation, not the date the appraiser inspects the property. It is imperative that your appraiser not use home sales that occurred following the date of separation as comps for the subject property since such sales would not have existed as of the date of separation.

Regarding household goods and furnishings, most cases do not involve personal property that is valuable enough to warrant a formal appraisal. In such cases, you can testify about what the items are worth. The fair market value of the household goods must be established, which is typically "Craigslist" or "garage sale" value, not purchase price or replacement value. Insurance appraisals can be tricky. If the other side tries to introduce an insurance appraisal to establish the value of personal property, your lawyer will want to point out that the insurance appraisal is reflective of replacement value, not fair market value.

Unequal Distribution

Once the court has identified the property, classified it as marital, divisible or separate, and valued the marital and divisible property, the court will distribute the marital and divisible property between the spouses. The equitable distribution statutes provide that there shall be an equal division of marital and divisible property unless the court determines that an equal division is not equitable; thus, in some cases, you may be able to ask for more than fifty percent of the property. NCGS § 50-20(c) sets forth the twelve statutory factors you can use to request an unequal distribution of marital and divisible property:

1. The income, property, and debts of each party at the time the property and debts are divided.
2. Any prior support obligations.
3. The duration of the marriage and the age and health of both parties.
4. The need of a parent with custody of the children to reside in the marital residence.
5. The expectation of retirement benefits that are not marital property.
6. Contribution made to the acquisition of marital property by the party not having title, including joint efforts or expenditures and contributions and services, or lack thereof, as a spouse, parent, wage earner, or homemaker.
7. Contributions made by one spouse to help educate or develop the career potential of the other spouse.
8. Any direct contribution to an increase in the value of separate property that occurs during the marriage.
9. The liquid or nonliquid character of the property.
10. The difficulty of valuing any business interests and the desirability of keeping the business intact and free from interference by the other party.
11. The tax consequences to each party.
11a. Acts of either party to preserve or to waste marital property or divisible property following separation.

11b. In the event of the death of either party prior to the entry of the equitable distribution order:

    a. Property passing to the surviving spouse by will or through intestacy.

    b. Property held as tenants by the entirety or as joint tenants with rights of survivorship.

    c. Property passing to the surviving spouse from life insurance or retirement accounts due to the death of a spouse.

    d. The surviving spouse's right to claim an "elective share" pursuant to NCGS § 30-3.1 through § 30-33.

12. Any other factor that the court finds proper.[54]

It is important to note that the North Carolina Supreme Court has held that a party desiring an unequal division of marital property bears not only the burden of producing evidence concerning one or more of the twelve factors in the statute, but also the burden of proving by a preponderance of the evidence that an equal division would not be equitable.[55]

Impact of Infidelity on Distribution

Unless a spouse committed some sort of financial misconduct, whether or not he or she committed adultery will have no bearing on the property distribution. While cheating on your spouse may lead to a divorce, it doesn't necessarily mean that you lose all of your rights and the other spouse automatically gets the kids, the house, and all the assets. In fact, the only claim to which infidelity is directly relevant is alimony.

In North Carolina, in order to be entitled to alimony, there must be a dependent spouse, meaning a spouse who is dependent on the other for financial needs, and a supporting spouse, meaning that spouse supports the other spouse and is more or less the breadwinner in the family. If the dependent spouse commits adultery, that spouse is barred from receiving alimony. Likewise, if the supporting spouse commits adultery, that spouse shall pay alimony. In North Carolina, alimony is slightly punitive with regard to cheating. For a more complete discussion of the ins and outs of alimony, see chapter 7.

Unless a spouse committed some sort of financial misconduct, whether or not he or she committed adultery will have no bearing on the property distribution.

While adultery is not directly relevant to the division of marital and divisible property, if marital assets are dissipated by the affair, such as the spouse spending money on the other party involved in the affair, then this "marital waste" is relevant and can be a factor for the judge to consider in the division of assets and debts. For example, if a spouse is spending money on a boyfriend or a girlfriend, in those cases the affair can be relevant to the extent that an argument can be made that the funds were spent for a nonmarital purpose. Obviously, spending money on an affair is not for the purpose of the marriage. If you can prove your spouse is spending money for a nonmarital purpose, then you can try to get those funds brought back into the marital estate as if they still exist and ask that they be distributed to the spouse who used them. The result is that you would end up getting more of the property that actually still exists. So in that respect, adultery can be relevant to an equitable distribution claim, but it's not the act of adultery per se. It's the marital resources that have been spent on a third party that should not have been spent for a nonmarital purpose.

The Family Business

"The Family Business" section is based on season 2, episode 1, of the podcast with my law partner Nicole Taylor.

As discussed above, in North Carolina generally speaking, marital property is any property acquired by either spouse from the day they got married until the day they separate from one another. There are a couple of exceptions for inheritances and gifts from third parties, but for the most part, property acquired during the marriage will likely be considered marital property and subject to division during a divorce. Given the large percentage of private and family-owned businesses in the United States and the fact that about half of American marriages end in divorce, it is important to understand what can happen to the family business in a divorce.

In general, the first thing you need to do is to get organized. In particular, if there is going to be an issue about any separate versus marital component of the business because you owned or acquired some portion of your interest before the marriage or by gift during the marriage, you will want to gather all the basic corporate documents, such as the articles of incorporation, any shareholder agreements or operating agreements, and any amendments to those agreements. Oftentimes these agreements haven't been reviewed in years, and you need to be sure to pull them back out and review them because they could have some key provisions regarding what happens to the business in the event of a divorce. For example, a divorce might trigger another shareholder's or partner's right to buy you out if your spouse names the company as a defendant in the lawsuit.

In addition, you should review your loans and lines of credit because there might be something in your loan covenants that could be triggered if your business is named as a defendant in a lawsuit. Knowing up front what the implications are is much better than trying to figure out and scramble after the fact once your business has been brought into the lawsuit. Another issue that can arise involves how to structure a distributive award payout. If you are the spouse keeping the business and will be using the income stream from the business to pay a distributive award over time, you have to make sure whatever money you will be distributing to yourself to pay your ex-spouse doesn't violate loan covenants to the bank. Most of the time, those covenants deal with what percentage of your net profits you can distribute out each year. Similarly, if you're trying the case in front of a judge, the judge needs to know the business owner's ability to pay.

You will also want to make sure that your business books are in order. A lot of times in a family-owned business where one spouse has always been the 100 percent shareholder, personal expenses may have been run through the business on a regular basis. If family expenses are being paid through the business, it needs to be done in a way where it is clear that the money came out of the business as income, or in some other fashion, to the business owner or for his or her benefit and not as trying to claim something as a business expense when it's clearly not. For example, when you're paying an expense using a check from the business bank account and the accountant codes it as a distribution, that's typically not problematic, because at the end of the day it's being accounted for. It is more problematic when a business owner is using the business credit card for both personal and business purposes, and then just paying the credit card off and coding the entire payment as a business expense.

It is very difficult after the fact to go back to the business credit card and try to figure out what expenses on the card are business expenses and what expenses are personal expenses. It can be an added layer of expense for the CPA or forensic accountant to go back through and try to allocate personal to business from those cards. In addition, everything changes once you start going through a divorce.

Making sure that your books are reliable might add a level of expense on the front end because you might have to pay a CPA to assist you. Then on the backend, in court or during settlement negotiations, you will be in a much better position if you have credible books and records.

You should also be wary of making big changes in your business while you are going through a divorce. Sometimes a legitimate business opportunity that you can't pass up may present itself. But if you have a controlling interest and you're going through a divorce and all of a sudden start making really big changes with your business—such as selling off assets or taking on huge amounts of debt for reasons that don't really appear to make good financial sense for a company— the other party may seek to join the business as a party to the lawsuit and ask the court to restrain you from taking any action that may negatively impact the value of the business. The court can potentially tie up your business by ordering that you can't buy or sell property or even take money out of your business bank account.

If you are the non-business owner spouse (often referred to as the "out spouse"), you need to try to get a handle on the business information. For the out spouse, it's often hard to do that before attorneys get involved because you might not have access to any of that information. Sometimes, however, you can at least get somewhat familiar with the income of the business by looking at your income tax returns if you file joint returns with your spouse.

The most important tip for anyone going through a divorce where a business interest is involved, whether you're the business owner or the "out spouse": go see a lawyer.

The most important tip for anyone going through a divorce where a business interest is involved, whether you're the business owner or the out spouse: go see a lawyer. You need to understand what implications the divorce may have for the business and what a divorce could mean for your family, particularly where the business is the main source of the family income.

How is the family business distributed?

Broadly speaking, there are three ways the business can be distributed. The first and most common way for the business to be distributed is to only one of the spouses. It is not unusual for the value of that business to far exceed most, if not all, the other marital assets. In such cases, typically one spouse receives the business and maybe a few of the smaller assets, and the other spouse receives the remaining marital property. If there are not sufficient other assets to equalize the distribution, the spouse receiving the business will most likely end up paying a distributive award to the other spouse.[56]

Alternatively, if the business is not distributed to one of the spouses, both spouses could continue to own an interest in the business. For example, if both spouses already owned an interest in the closely held business while they were married, sometimes the only way to divide the marital estate is for the parties to continue to co-own the business. You don't often see this scenario, however, because judges really want to help the parties disentangle their finances. Continuing to co-own a business with your ex-spouse brings about its own set of problems.

If you continue to be business partners with your ex-spouse, in essence, you can experience the same problems that you might have with any other business partner, but the situation is exacerbated because you are dealing with your ex-spouse with whom you already have trust issues. For example, the two of you might disagree about how or when the profits should be distributed, how much each of you should be paid in salary, whether there should be a capital call, or whether to take out loans to either expand or cover expenses during an economic downturn. People get separated and divorced for a reason, so if you are already distrustful of your ex-spouse and then find yourself having to co-own and run a business with them, it can be challenging to say the least. One way that you can try to reduce the amount of conflict you might have down the road with your ex-spouse and business partner is to hire a corporate lawyer to help draft shareholder or operating agreements that address and create rules for managing the various scenarios that can arise.

The third way the business can be distributed in a divorce is to sell the business or interest in the business and then agree on how the proceeds will be divided. Of the three options for distributing the business, selling the business is the least common. Just like agreeing to co-ownership following a separation, agreeing to sell the business and divide the proceeds brings its own set of potential challenges. Again, consider bringing in a business lawyer for input on what kind of language to include in the agreement regarding the terms of a sale, how decisions will be made, and how conflict will be resolved. If the parties can't agree or get into an argument about the logistics of the sale or how to implement it, or ultimately what terms to accept, your agreement should have specific language on how disputes will be settled.

How will my business be valued?

Assuming that the business will be distributed to one of the parties, the business will need to be valued. The easiest, although not necessarily the smartest way for the business to be valued, is for the parties to agree on what the business is worth. In most cases, however, agreeing upon the value of the business is challenging, and it is rare that parties will agree right from the start. With that said, it can happen in situations where both spouses have an in-depth understanding and knowledge of the business and both feel comfortable that they have a good handle on what the business is probably worth. Another situation in which the parties may be able to agree upon the value of the business is where there has been a recent offer to purchase the business.

If the separating couple cannot agree, they will need to bring in an expert business appraiser to value the business. The parties can each get their own expert, or they can, on occasion, agree to use a joint expert, meaning they would retain that person jointly to prepare the appraisal to be used for purposes of trying to negotiate their settlement. Once the expert or experts have been hired and the financial information and documents about the company have been exchanged, the expert will consider three different approaches to value the business.

The first approach is based on the company's assets minus the company's debts, basically a balance-sheet approach. The second approach is based on income—what the future expectations for an investor would be if the person were going to invest in the company. There are several methods that fall under the income approach. The business appraiser could look at the income of the company and project what an investor would expect to receive as an income stream, and they can capitalize the earnings. The appraiser can also do a discounted cashflow method.

The third method is the market-based approach, which involves looking at similar companies in the same geographical region to find comparable sales to arrive at the value. The market approach is similar to real estate valuation, where you look at market comps for homes in the area to try to see what the value of your home might be. Likewise, the business appraiser would do the same thing for market sales on stocks of companies that are similar in nature and in the same geographic region as the particular company being valued. The market approach can be difficult since a lot of times no sales are comparable or, for the comps that do exist, not enough information is available to make any necessary adjustments. For example, a lot of times the business valuator is reviewing information for publicly traded companies that have revenues 100 times more than the small, closely held business they are valuing. Pursuant to their business valuation standards, business valuators are required to go through the exercise of using all three approaches, but most of the time they rely primarily, if not solely, on what the income approach indicates is the value of the company.

What date will the business appraiser use to value my business?

For purposes of equitable distribution, property is valued as of the date of separation. As we discussed in chapter 1, the date of separation is the date that the parties physically stopped living in the same house with the intent of at least one of them that the separation be permanent. Sometimes if the business will have to be valued as of other dates as well. For example, if the business was owned by one of the parties prior to marriage, you might also need to value the business on the date of marriage, because there may be a question as to whether the business has a separate component. In order to determine whether there is a separate component, you would have to determine the value of the business on the date of marriage, as well as the value of the business on the date of separation, and to the extent that there was any increase in value during that time period you have to consider what caused that increase in value. Passive increases in value to a separate asset occurring during the marriage remains separate property, but if there's an active increase in value to that separate asset, the active increase in value can be marital property. As a result, someone's shares in a company that they owned prior to marriage may be a mixed asset containing both marital and separate components depending on whether there is a change in value.

One key difference between postseparation support and alimony, is that adultery on the part of the dependent spouse will not necessarily bar their claim for postseparation support.

CHAPTER 7

Postseparation Support and Alimony

In many marriages, one spouse is financially dependent upon the other spouse for support. Maybe one parent stays home with the children while the other parent works outside of the home. In those situations, what happens when the couple separates? How does the dependent spouse pay their bills? The answer is postseparation support and alimony.

Postseparation Support

Postseparation support is spousal support to be paid until one of the following occurs: a termination date specified in the court order; entry of an order awarding or denying alimony; dismissal of the alimony claim; entry of a divorce judgment if no alimony claim is pending; the cohabitation or remarriage of the party

Postseparation support is spousal support to be paid until one of the following occurs: a termination date specified in the court order; entry of an order awarding or denying alimony; dismissal of the alimony claim; entry of a divorce judgment if no alimony claim is pending; the cohabitation or remarriage of the party receiving postseparation support; or the death of either party.

receiving postseparation support; or the death of either party.[57] At a very basic level, postseparation support can be thought of as "temporary alimony." In ordering postseparation support, the court will base its award on the financial needs of the parties considering their accustomed standard of living, current incomes, and expenses.[58]

No particular formula is used to determine the amount of postseparation support that is appropriate, and the analysis will be similar to the analysis described in the following section with respect to calculating alimony payments. One key difference between postseparation support and alimony, is that adultery on the part of the dependent spouse will not necessarily bar their claim for postseparation support.[59] While the court will consider acts of marital misconduct committed by the dependent spouse in making its determination as to whether to award postseparation support, an act of adultery by the dependent spouse will not automatically bar their claim.

Alimony

North Carolina defines alimony as "an order for payment for the support and maintenance of a spouse or former spouse."[60] Who pays it? How is it calculated? What factors influence how much alimony one receives? The answers aren't as straight-forward as you might think. In general, alimony exists to create two financially comparable households upon separation. Alimony can be traced back to the Babylonian Code of Hammurabi, which obligated a man who divorced his wife to provide an allowance to sustain her needs and those of their children.

While some argue that alimony, with its Babylonian roots, is an antiquated concept, the process of determining alimony payments has clearly evolved along with society. By evaluating the financial needs and assets of both parties, and even accounting for situations involving marital misconduct, the process for determining alimony is typically grounded in fairness and equality.

Alimony is paid by the supporting spouse to the dependent spouse. The supporting spouse is the spouse upon whom the other spouse is substantially dependent for support or from whom the other spouse is in need of support to maintain his or her accustomed standard of living. Sometimes the supporting spouse is the husband, and sometimes it's the wife. Typically, the determination of who is the supporting spouse is decided based on the incomes of both parties at the time of separation.

If the parties are able to resolve their issues outside of court, they can determine the details of any alimony payments in a separation agreement. These details include which spouse will pay alimony to the other, the amount of the alimony payments, and the duration of those payments. If the case goes to court, a judge will determine whether one spouse is a supporting spouse, whether the other spouse is a dependent spouse, how much money the dependent spouse will receive each month, and for what length of time.

North Carolina law does not provide a formula for calculating alimony, but the process typically involves several rules of thumb. Again, if the couple resolves their issues out of court in a separation agreement, they determine the amount and duration of alimony payments through discussions with their divorce attorneys and, most likely, some degree of compromise. If the case goes to court, however, the spouse requesting alimony must prove to the court that they are a dependent spouse and that the other is a supporting spouse. In order to make that determination, the court will consider factors such as the dependent spouse's budget and income, the amount of child support the dependent spouse receives, and how much alimony the dependent spouse needs to meet their monthly budget, taking income and child support payments into consideration.

The analysis doesn't stop there. Once the dependent spouse's need for alimony is determined, the court must consider the supporting spouse's ability to pay alimony, taking into consideration the supporting spouse's budget and income. In many cases, there is simply not enough money to go around since it costs more money to support two households. Thus, the supporting spouse may not have the ability to pay the amount of alimony needed by the dependent spouse to meet their budget. In such cases, the alimony award will likely be less than what the dependent spouse believes is needed.

Just as there is no formula for calculating the amount of monthly alimony payment amounts, there is no formula for calculating the duration of the payments. One rule of thumb is that the dependent spouse is likely to receive alimony for half the length of the marriage. For example, if the couple was married for ten years, the supporting spouse would pay alimony for five years. With that said, this rule of thumb is not a requirement, and it is up to the parties and their divorce attorneys— or the judge—to determine. In some limited circumstances, lifetime alimony may be appropriate; however, it is not the norm.

How does marital misconduct impact alimony?

Marital misconduct is relevant in setting the alimony payment. A dependent spouse who commits adultery is barred from receiving alimony in the state of North Carolina. Likewise, a supporting spouse who commits adultery must pay alimony. In North Carolina cases involving adultery, alimony can be used punitively, and the act of adultery can affect both the amount and the duration of alimony payments. Other forms of

A dependent spouse who commits adultery is barred from receiving alimony in the state of North Carolina. Likewise, a supporting spouse who commits adultery must pay alimony.

marital misconduct may also be relevant to the analysis, although they won't bar an alimony claim altogether, as is the case with adultery. These other forms of marital misconduct include, among other things, indignities (such as name-calling and public humiliation), excessive use of alcohol and drugs, reckless spending, cruel and barbarous treatment (including domestic violence or any type of physical abuse), and abandonment.

How can I tell if my spouse is cheating?

Cheating, or adultery as it's often referred to, is one of the more challenging problems that can arise in a marriage, and often it is one of the factors associated with the decision to separate or divorce. As a divorce attorney, there are several signs I often see that may indicate a spouse is cheating. Note that these signs alone and collectively do not constitute concrete evidence of an affair, and you need actual facts to substantiate a legal allegation of adultery. But if you suspect such behavior, you may want to consider and then follow up on these signs.

First and foremost, the spouse suspected of cheating often exhibits a sudden change in behavior. If they have acted a certain way throughout the marriage, most likely these actions are not an indication of cheating;

but if they suddenly begin engaging in behavior that is out of character, this change in behavior may be an indication of infidelity. Excuses to be away from the home and family activities can also be an indicator of infidelity. If your spouse suddenly has to work a lot of overtime for no apparent reason, or is scheduled to go on multiple business trips when they normally do not travel for work, they may have a paramour waiting in the wings. Being overly protective of their cell phone or excessively using the Internet and social media can also be an indication of cheating. If your spouse has begun leaving the room to take phone calls, suddenly has a passcode on their phone and is constantly clearing their Internet browser history, they may be cheating. If you ask to use your spouse's cell phone, and they make up an excuse as to why you can't use it, or your spouse watches you like a hawk while you are using it, there may be a problem.

Changes in physical appearance or sex drive may also be indicators that your spouse is having an affair. New hairstyles, new clothes, or a sudden obsession with going to the gym or losing weight may mean there is a third party in the picture. The lack of interest in sex may also mean that your spouse is cheating. When a person is engaging in an affair, they may act repulsed by the touch of their spouse. Small acts of affection such as hugs or kisses or even placing your hand on your spouse's knee may result in your spouse pushing you away from them. Your spouse may also try to initiate arguments with you for seemingly no reason at all.

In most cases when you confront your partner with accusations of cheating, they may deny it and make you feel bad for not trusting them. Or worse, they may insinuate that you are the one who is being unfaithful.

If I suspect my spouse is cheating, what can I do?

Evidence of adultery can be crucial to your case if you or your spouse has a potential alimony claim. In North Carolina, a dependent spouse who commits adultery is barred from receiving alimony, whereas a supporting spouse who commits adultery is required to pay alimony. Evidence of adultery or other marital misconduct occurring after the separation can only be used to corroborate evidence of marital misconduct occurring during the marriage and prior to separation. Thus, if you suspect your spouse may be cheating, you need to gather this evidence before either you or your spouse moves out of the home. One way that you can collect this evidence is to hire a private investigator (PI) to assist you.

In addition to hiring a PI, a good source of information to collect with regard to your spouse's extramarital activities can be emails. However, while electronic evidence of marital misconduct can be very important to your case, remember that there is a right way and a wrong way to go about collecting your evidence. If your spouse uses a computer to which you know the password, you may, under certain circumstances, be able to access his or her emails. However, beware that it is illegal to obtain information by installing a keylogger, a keystroke device, or any other spyware program on your spouse's computer. If you illegally intercept your spouse's emails, not only will your evidence be inadmissible in court, but also your spouse may also have a claim against you for wiretapping. The same goes for recording your spouse's telephone or other conversations. North Carolina is a one-party state, meaning that only one party to the conversation has to consent to its recording, and you can be that party if you are in fact participating in the conversation. You can't, however, install a device on your home phone or your spouse's cell phone that records every incoming and outcoming phone call. If you did that, those actions may be considered wiretapping.

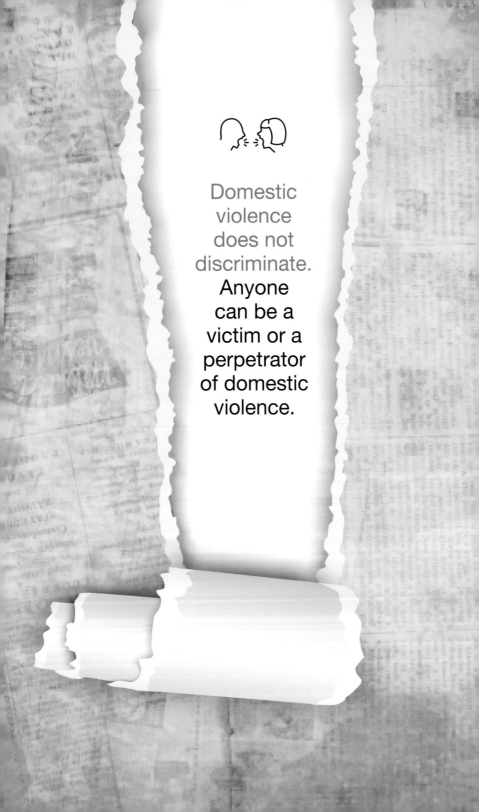

Domestic violence does not discriminate.
Anyone can be a victim or a perpetrator of domestic violence.

CHAPTER 8

Domestic Violence

This chapter is based on season 1, episode 16, of the podcast with my law partner Jonathan Melton.

Domestic violence does not discriminate. Anyone can be a victim or a perpetrator of domestic violence. It transcends all socioeconomic boundaries and education levels and can affect people of any race, age, sexual orientation, religion, or gender. Domestic violence can happen to people who are married, who are living together, or who are dating.

If you are a victim of domestic violence, you can seek a domestic violence protective order, also referred to as a DVPO or 50B order (because it is defined in North Carolina General Statutes Chapter 50B). In order to obtain a DVPO, you must prove that someone has attempted to cause you bodily injury, has in fact caused you bodily injury, or has placed you or a member of your family in fear of serious bodily injury or in fear of continued harassment that rises to such a level as to cause emotional distress.

You are eligible to file for a DVPO if you are current or former spouses with the person who you believe has caused domestic violence; if you are members of the opposite sex who live together or have lived together; if you are related to the person as parents and children, or grandparents and children; if you have a child in common with the person; if you are current or former household members; or if you are in an opposite-sex dating relationship.[61] It is important to note that the statute only protects opposite-sex dating relationships. If you are in a same-sex dating relationship, you will not be able to get a domestic violence order of protection unless you can fall into one of the other protected relationship categories, such as having lived together.

Behaviors That Can Lead to a DVPO

Many types of behaviors can enable you to seek a DVPO. Anything that causes you to suffer a physical injury, such as being hit, kicked, pushed, or choked, will enable you to seek a DVPO. In addition, any behavior that causes you to be scared of imminent bodily injury will also enable you to seek a DVPO. Bear in mind that it is a subjective fear. If someone threatens you, and you believe that you are actually going to be hurt, that threat could enable you to seek a domestic violence order of protection.

The question is whether or not the person being threatened is fearful, not whether an objective third party would be scared. If you are scared, then you may be able to seek a DVPO. In trying to assess a person's subjective fear, judges will often look at the history or a pattern between the two individuals involved in the action. The history that the victim has with the person they believe is causing domestic violence may be important to understanding why that specific person is afraid in that specific circumstance. Continued harassment can also give you grounds to seek a DVPO. In such cases, the court will look at an aggregate of behaviors, such as excessive text messages, telephone calls, emails, or following or otherwise "stalking" someone.

If you think that you need a DVPO, it is important that you take action right away. Typically, the longer someone waits to seek a protective order, the more stale the incident in question becomes, and the more difficult it will be to get the protective order. As discussed above, the history between the two individuals is relevant; thus, if there is a recent act of domestic violence between the parties, the judge will take into consideration evidence of old acts, or evidence of a pattern or a history of abuse. In most cases, however, the judge cannot base the domestic violence order of protection on an old act or on the history of abuse. There has to be a recent act of domestic violence between the parties.

If there is not a domestic violence office in your county, the clerk's office should have the forms available for you.

Procedure for Obtaining a DVPO

If you are a resident of North Carolina and you would like to seek a DVPO, the first step is to file a civil court action by completing a Complaint and Motion for Domestic Violence Protective Order form. In many counties, a domestic violence office at the courthouse has the forms available. If there is not a domestic violence office in your county, the clerk's office should have the forms available for you. There is no filing fee associated with seeking a DVPO.

If you happen to live in Wake County, agencies like Interact assist victims of domestic violence. They will even assist you with completing the necessary forms to file your domestic violence action. Wake County also has a domestic violence office that maintains all of the forms. The Wake County domestic violence office is located on the fifth floor of the Wake County Courthouse adjacent to Courtroom 5A where the actions for protective orders are considered.

Once you have completed and filed the complaint form, the judge will review your complaint and the allegations you included, and the judge may ask you some questions. If the judge thinks based on the allegations you included in the complaint, and based on some of the limited questions they may ask you, that you have grounds for a domestic violence protective order, that judge can issue an ex parte (which means without notice to the defendant) emergency temporary order. If the judge issues the emergency temporary order, when you leave the courthouse that day, you will have an enforceable DVPO. The opposing party will then be served with your complaint and with the emergency order.

Once the opposing party defendant is served, they are constitutionally entitled to have a hearing within ten days. At the full hearing, the defendant will get to tell their side of the story, and you will be present as well to tell the court your version of the events that transpired. If based on the evidence presented, the judge believes that the defendant committed an act of domestic violence against you, the judge will enter the domestic violence protective order, which will stay in effect for one year. Before the expiration of the DVPO, you can file a motion asking the court to renew the DVPO for an additional two years. You can ask for a renewal even if you don't live in North Carolina anymore, and you don't need new facts for a renewal, but having new facts can be helpful. For example, if there is a new act of domestic violence or a violation of the existing order, it will help your chances for renewal, but technically the judge can renew the DVPO based on the underlying facts from the initial order.

Provisions Typically included in a DVPO

The DVPO will have provisions that are specific to the alleged victim and typically includes provisions as to where the person who committed domestic violence can and cannot go. For example, you can ask the judge to order that the defendant can't go to your house or your place of work or that they can't come within fifty to 100 yards of you. In addition, the defendant will not be allowed to contact you by phone, text, email, or otherwise. The defendant is also prohibited from contacting you through a third party. They cannot contact a friend and ask them to pass along a message to you. That would be a violation of the DVPO. One exception is that if the parties are represented by counsel, the lawyers are permitted to contact one another to discuss the case.

In some cases where the parties have children together, the parties may be permitted to communicate with one another to discuss logistics with respect to the children. Usually, these communications will be limited to writings such as emails or text messages. In the DVPO, the judge can also include provisions that the defendant will have no contact with you unless it is in writing and only concerning the children's well-being or the logistics of the custody schedule.

In connection with a DVPO, you can request possession of a shared household, for possession of automobiles, and for temporary custody of children and pets. You can also request temporary support and attorney's fees. Bear in mind, however, if these provisions are included in your protective order, they are not permanent since the DVPO will expire at some point. In most cases, you will have to take further steps in regular family court to get more permanent relief, but on a limited, temporary basis, you can ask for all of that relief.

Evidence for Your Hearing

First and foremost, if you experience an incident of domestic violence, call the police. Not only will calling the police help ensure your safety, but also it will help create a record to document the incident.

First and foremost, if you experience an incident of domestic violence, call the police. Not only will calling the police help ensure your safety, but also it will help create a record to document the incident. If the police file a report, you may be able to use the report at the hearing on your claim for a domestic violence protective order. In addition, your own testimony is going to be your best evidence. You will be your best witness, and you need to tell the judge exactly what happened. Describe it fully both in the form complaint and when you are testifying. Be very clear about what you felt and what the person looked like during the incident. Since the fear you must prove is your subjective fear, the judge needs to be able to feel like they are where you were at that moment.

Other people who witnessed the incident or witnessed your behavior right after the incident are also helpful. If someone can testify as to how upset you were or how injured you were, they can be helpful to your case. Photographs are also good evidence. Take pictures of your actual injuries if you suffered any injuries. Also photograph any destruction to your home. Since the judge will be looking for evidence of imminent serious bodily injury, having photographs showing where the opposing party has punched holes in walls, broken windows, or ripped doors off hinges can be good evidence for your case.

Remember that obtaining a domestic violence protective order is a civil court action, and in most civil court actions, it is going to be your word against the opposing party's word. If you tell a close family member or friend what is happening to you, that person can be a witness. If you tell the police, that police officer can be a witness for you and will have a police report. If you have photographs of destruction to your home or your property or of your injuries, the evidence can be helpful to support your version of the events that transpired. Threatening text messages, voicemails, and emails should all be preserved and brought to the hearing when you are seeking a domestic violence protective order.

Removing the Other Person from the Home

Once the emergency order is entered, the sheriff's department will show up and remove the person from the home. They will be allowed to gather their personal effects, which usually consists of clothes, toiletries, and tools of the trade such as their computer or other items they need for work. The person will have a short amount of time to remove these things and then will be removed from the home. At that point, they will not be allowed back into the home until a judge orders otherwise. If the person remaining in the home has the locks changed and claims that the person who was removed from the home has established a separate residence, it could be very difficult for the person who was removed to get back into the home at all. This is one of the reasons why these actions are taken so seriously by our judges. For two individuals who may be married, living together, and have children, one of the spouses can acquire a big advantage in their domestic family court action by getting the other spouse removed from the house this way. Judges are mindful of this fact and try to make sure that a person is not filing for a domestic violence protective order for an improper purpose.

Consent Orders

Consent orders usually happen in one of two ways. If you obtain an ex parte emergency order and then everyone comes back to court for the return hearing, before the return hearing when everyone is gathered, you can attempt to reach a consent order with the other side without having to go before the judge. Alternatively, if the judge does not think you have grounds for the emergency order, they can set a hearing on your complaint for a domestic violence protective order. Prior to the hearing, you can negotiate a consent domestic

A domestic violence protective order, just like any other court order, is a piece of paper, but unlike other court orders, if a person violates a DVPO they are automatically charged criminally.

violence protective order with the opposing side.

The benefit to negotiating a consent order is that you can agree the order will include no findings of fact or conclusions of law. If you are the alleged abuser, if you consent to a domestic violence protective order with no findings and no conclusions, the order itself won't say what you did or did not do, and you are not admitting any guilt. Depending on what a person does for a living, having a DVPO entered could cause the person to lose their job. If you are able to resolve the issue with a consent order, the victim gets the relief they are seeking, and the alleged perpetrator is able to protect their employment by not admitting to any wrongdoing. Such a situation can be a win-win for both parties in cases where the victim relies on the income of the opposing party for support.

Violations of the DVPO

A domestic violence protective order, just like any other court order, is a piece of paper, but unlike other court orders, if a person violates a DVPO they are automatically charged criminally. If the opposing party violates the DVPO, it is a class A1 misdemeanor. If they violate the DVPO more than two times, it is a felony. If you have a valid domestic violence protective order and a violation occurs, call the police, and the defendant will be arrested and charged. If you obtain a DVPO, you cannot give permission to the other party to violate the DVPO. In fact, even if you contact the person and tell them it is OK to come to your house, if the person who has the DVPO against them goes to the victim's house, they will be arrested if the violation is reported. If you have a DVPO in place and you decide that you don't want it to be in effect anymore, you will need to file a motion with the court and ask the judge to set the order aside. Judges take these motions very seriously because they don't want individuals who have obtained domestic violence protective orders to be coerced by the perpetrator into setting the order aside. A hearing will be scheduled, and the judge will ask the victim why they do not want the DVPO to be in place anymore.

Firearms

If the person against whom you are seeking a DVPO owns firearms, you can ask the judge to take the person's firearms. If the judge orders the weapons to be surrendered, they must be turned in immediately to the sheriff's department upon service of the DVPO or within twenty-four hours of service at a time and place specified by the sheriff.[62] After the DVPO expires, the defendant can file a motion for the return of their weapons. The motion for return of firearms must be filed within ninety days of the DVPO's expiration, and a hearing will be held. At the hearing, the judge will consider any other domestic violence protective orders against the defendant, how many times the order may have been renewed, whether the defendant has any pending criminal charges, or any other reason why they are prohibited from possessing firearms. With none of these findings, the person will get their guns back.

50C Orders

If you do not fall within one of the protected relationships outlined in North Carolina General Statutes chapter 50B that would enable you to seek a domestic violence protective order, you might be able to seek a civil no contact order pursuant to chapter 50C, also called a 50C order. In order to obtain a 50C order, you have to prove that the opposing party committed unlawful conduct against you. The statute defines unlawful conduct as nonconsensual sexual conduct and stalking. Stalking is further defined as following or otherwise harassing another person on more than one occasion without any legal purpose with the intent to place the person in reasonable fear of their safety or to cause the person substantial emotional distress.[63]

To reach the stalking prong of the statute, a high level of communication is needed. Typically, the court will consider an aggregate of contact. A couple of text messages over a couple of days will likely not rise to the level necessary to obtain a 50C order, but hundreds of text messages over a couple of days might. Other behavior that could enable you seek a

50C order includes someone parking in front of your home, looking in your windows, contacting your boss, contacting your friends, or contacting your neighbors. These are all actions that a reasonable person would likely find substantially, emotionally distressful. The procedure for seeking a 50C order is substantially the same as for seeking a domestic violence protective order. Again, you will fill out a complaint form, and the judge will review it. If the judge thinks you have included enough allegations in the complaint that would warrant the issuance of a 50C order, they will issue a temporary ex parte order that will be valid for up to ten days. A return hearing will be scheduled, and as with a domestic violence protective order, the defendant to a 50C action will have the opportunity to be heard and to present their side of the story to the court.

The most striking difference with a domestic violence protective order and a 50C order is with respect to how the two orders can be enforced. When a person violates a DVPO, they are arrested. A 50C Order can only be enforced by civil or criminal contempt. No arrest or criminal charges are imminent. If the defendant violates the 50C order, the burden is on you to file a motion for civil or criminal contempt.

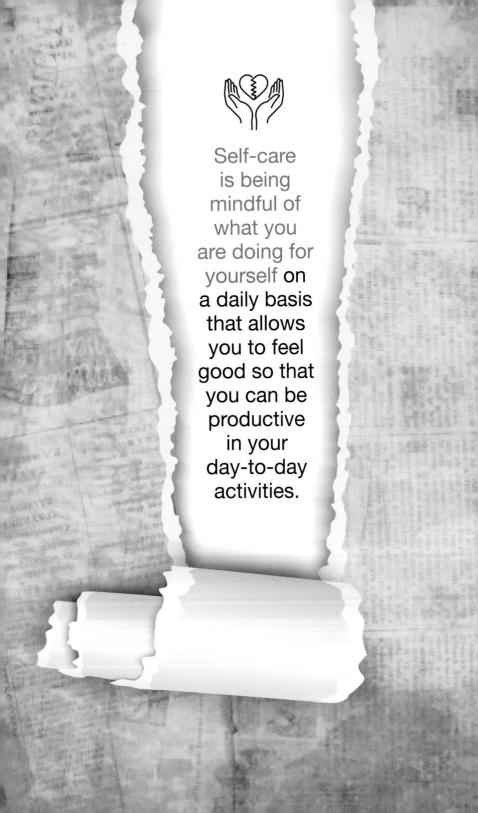

Self-care is being mindful of what you are doing for yourself on a daily basis that allows you to feel good so that you can be productive in your day-to-day activities.

CHAPTER 9

Self-Care

 This chapter is based on season 1, episode 13, of the podcast with fellow family law attorney Lynn McNally.

As you near the end of this book, you are probably aware that you need to consider the legal implications of your current marital situation. But have you considered how you will take care of yourself as you navigate this process? Your divorce involves more than how the law will apply to the facts of your particular case, which is for the lawyers to address. The most important part for you to address is how you will thrive. Clients often come to their divorce lawyers ready to discuss the facts of their cases, but they aren't physically and mentally prepared to go through the divorce process.

To make it through a divorce, you have to stay healthy. And in order to stay healthy, in my experience, you need to practice really good self-care. Self-care is being mindful of what you are doing for yourself on a daily basis that allows you to feel good so that you can be productive in your day-to-day activities.

You need to consider both your emotional health and physical health. In the context of a divorce, emotional health encompasses the ability to go through the grieving process in a way that is productive. Grieving will likely look different for each person. As discussed in chapter 3, for many people, going through a divorce is much like dealing with the death of a loved one, and you will likely experience the various stages of grief at different points during the divorce process. If you are not cognizant of that fact and don't try to develop an understanding of what is going on with your emotions, you might have a really hard time getting through it.

Many people going through a divorce need someone to help them process their feelings. Sometimes that person is a friend, and sometimes it is a family member. Other times, it is necessary to have a professional such as a counselor or a therapist help you process those feelings. In my experience, you can't be emotionally healthy until you have had an opportunity to feel the feelings and work through them in a productive way. When you are starting the divorce process, so many unanswered questions swirl around you. How am I going to make financial ends meet?

What am I going do when I don't have the children on Christmas day? So many unknowns can send you into a tailspin. Thus, it is important to have someone who can help you work through your feelings and give you tools to manage those stressful and anxious emotions as they arise.

Recognizing that you have an issue that you would like to address in a constructive way is actually a good thing. You will be viewed as someone who can recognize a problem, find the resources to help you resolve the problem, and then move on in a positive way.

Sometimes clients are worried they will be penalized by a judge or by the opposing party if they seek help from a therapist. Recognizing that you have an issue that you would like to address in a constructive way is actually a good thing. You will be viewed as someone who can recognize a problem, find the resources to help you resolve the problem, and then move on in a positive way. In my experience, family court judges do not hold it against people when they seek the help they need during the divorce process. The bigger issue is when clients do not recognize that they have an issue and don't get the help they need. Instead of therapy, maybe the person starts self-medicating by turning to alcohol or drugs or some other destructive behavior. At the end of the day, this type of behavior will be a much bigger detriment, especially if you are involved in a custody case. If you think you would benefit from talk therapy or medication, I can't stress this point enough—get the help you need!

In addition to making sure that you get the help you need, be wary of comparing your situation to the divorce your friend or family member experienced. Almost everyone knows somebody who has gone through a divorce, and it can seem comforting to talk to somebody who is similarly situated because they know in some respects what you are going through. Unfortunately, it can also be incredibly unproductive. As we all know, misery loves company. Sometimes, talking to someone who has gone through or is currently going through a divorce can escalate your feelings on the subject. No two divorce cases are the same. It is nearly impossible for you to compare the facts of your case to anyone else's case.

Clients often ask why their friend might be getting a certain amount of child support each month while they aren't getting that much, but they haven't considered that the friend has a different number of children, a different custodial schedule, and the people's incomes are completely different. These situations are so fact specific, and your friend has likely not told you every single little detail that goes into the analysis of a child support calculation or whether a particular custody schedule is in the best interest of particular children. In addition, with the advent of social media and meet-up groups and online platforms where people who are going through a divorce can communicate with each other, you may not even know what state the person is in who is telling you about their divorce. Family law can vary greatly from state to state on these issues, so again, you just can't compare. The moral of the story is to connect with your friends in a positive way, but keep in mind that your case can't be compared to anyone else's case.

Dating Following Separation

In most cases, dating immediately following a separation is not a good idea, not just for the sake of your emotional health but also for plenty of other legal reasons. Jumping back into a relationship so quickly may not allow you the opportunity to fully process the emotions you have to deal with while going through the divorce. A large part of self-care is being mindful and being present. A new relationship, no matter how casual, can be distracting. Rather than processing the emotions you are feeling, you are using the new relationship to ignore them by putting all of your emotional focus on someone else. Instead of turning your focus toward yourself and saying, "What can I do to make myself feel better and to be better?" you are turning your efforts outward and trying to create a brand-new relationship with someone else. Remember that you only have so much energy. When you are going through the divorce process, you need to conserve your energy and keep your focus in order to make the difficult decisions that you will face.

In most cases, the divorce process is not a short one. A typical divorce in North Carolina is going to take at

There will be moments when you are navigating the divorce process when it is hard to see light at the end of the tunnel, and it is in those moments that an act of self-care, whatever that means to you, is the most important.

least a year and a day. You need to make sure you have the energy to make it through that year and get through the divorce. You will get through the process, and you will likely feel like a different person in twelve months. You can heal through the process, and you can come out better on the other side.

You just have to trust the process and do the work to get there. There's something kind of nice about getting a "do over" even if you liked the way things were the first time around with your marriage and didn't want to be separated. The reality of your situation is that you are separated, and you have this great opportunity to do whatever things you want to do with the rest of your life.

There will be moments when you are navigating the divorce process when it is hard to see light at the end of the tunnel, and it is in those moments that an act of self-care, whatever that means to you, is the most important. An act of self-care can be taking ten minutes to sit down and just breathe or writing in a journal or taking a walk outside and just sort of refocusing and being present. You need these mindful activities the most during the times when you just can't see the positive.

Why Taking Care of Your Emotional Health During a Divorce Is So Important

A family lawyer can do many things for their client, but some things we just cannot do for you. For example, I can't tell you what assets exist in your marital estate. I can't decide for you what custodial schedule you are willing to accept for your children, and I can't decide for you how much support you are willing to accept. These are just a few of the very important decisions that only my clients can make, and those clients who take care of their emotional health during the divorce process are better equipped to make good decisions in that regard. As a family law attorney, I am able to do more things, more efficiently for my clients who are healthy enough to engage with me actively in this process.

There is a danger when a person is newly separated that they will become paralyzed and unable to make even the smallest of decisions because of the anxiety and stress that being separated causes. Going through a divorce is a huge life change, and it is completely normal to feel these emotions, but the key is to find a way out of that particular situation, whether it's to take a walk or refocus or take prescribed medication. Whatever you need to do, you have to be able to move forward and put one foot in front of the other. At the beginning of the process, it can be helpful not to think big picture, because trying to figure out what your life will look like in a year or more can be very overwhelming. Early on in the divorce process, it will likely be easier to take it day by day and to baby step through each individual issue. Hopefully, by taking it one day at a time, you won't get overwhelmed in January with what the Christmas custodial schedule will be the following December. Think about what is going to happen tomorrow. Who has the children tomorrow? How are you going to pay this month's bills? You need to be able to get through the immediate issues first, and practicing acts of self-care can help you be able to work through these issues with your lawyer.

Pick Your Battles

As you are going through this process, you don't have to fight every battle with your spouse, and you shouldn't fight every battle. Clients who are cognizant of caring for their emotional health throughout the process are better equipped to pick their battles, and they are better able to let an issue go when it isn't going to advance their case. When you are going through a separation, you do not have to continue engaging your spouse in the acrimony that was the norm during your marriage. You can disengage from being in constant fight-or-flight mode and begin choosing your battles. Everything does not have to be an emergency. When folks are first beginning this process, there is a tendency to get stuck in fight-or-flight mode, and every little thing that happens sends you over the edge. Once you recognize that it doesn't have to be that way in and of itself is a huge step toward self-care.

Proactively Taking Care of Your Emotional Health During a Divorce

Figure out what you enjoy doing that also makes you feel healthy and make a point to do those things. Talking to people, whether a mental health professional or friends and family members, can help. There are many resources out there to help you take care of your mental health regardless of your financial situation, whether it's calling your insurance company and asking whom your in-network providers are or finding a trusted friend who is going to listen to you and not ramp you up. Maintaining good relationships with people and using those relationships where you can are both good steps to take to manage your emotional health. Meditation, journaling, reading, and even exercise can help you maintain your mental and emotional heath when you are going through a divorce.

Something else you can do to take care of your emotional health during a divorce is to make your home comfortable. If you are the person who stayed in the marital home while your spouse moved out but left all of their stuff there, pack it up and put it in a box if you just don't want to look at it anymore. Don't get rid of it—your lawyer will probably tell you that's a bad idea. But stick it in a box and put it in the garage or in a corner, somewhere you don't have to look at it anymore, and begin to make the home yours. If, on the other hand, you are the person who left and you are setting up a new household, get yourself some stuff that makes you feel good. Decorate your new home in a way that

> **Physical health and mental health are so interrelated that these kinds of things you do physically can either help clear your head or clutter it back up.**

you enjoy and that your spouse would have never agreed to let you do in the marital home.

Be organized and simplify things. You are going to be asked by your lawyers to put together an incredible amount of information. If you can approach that task in a step-by-step manner and develop a good understanding of what your assets and debts are and what the family income is and simplify that process in your own mind, it helps clear the clutter both literally and figuratively. Get yourself some file folders and organize those financial documents!

Taking Care of Your Physical Health During a Divorce

Taking care of your physical health during a divorce is also important. Don't forget to both eat and be mindful of what you eat. It is easy to become depressed during this process, and I see a lot of my clients lose weight. Most likely, it is not a healthy weight loss, so it's important to be mindful of what you are eating and to make sure you are eating enough. It is also important not to self-medicate. If you need medication, ask your doctor to prescribe medication for you for the amount of time that you need it. Don't take someone else's medication. Don't take old medication that was prescribed to you years ago. Don't medicate with alcohol. All of these things will lead to your mind being cluttered. Physical health and mental health are so interrelated that these kinds of things you do physically can either help clear your head or clutter it back up.

Exercise is important and can be as simple as taking some time to stretch, going for a walk, or working out at the gym. Whatever you choose to do, move your body and get some exercise. You also need to figure out how to sleep and sleep well. Hopefully, eating well, not self-medicating, and exercising will lead you to sleep restfully, but not sleeping well is another problem that my clients often experience during this process. Finally, find whatever activity you can that reduces stress for you. If there is an activity you have done in the past that makes you feel good—maybe you like to go to art class or maybe you belong to a running club or whatever the activity is—keep doing it. Don't let it fall by the wayside because you're going through a separation. The key is to find an activity that makes you feel good long term and not just something that makes you feel good for the moment.

Your Team

One strategy for accomplishing your self-care goals, whatever they are, is to put them in writing and then share that writing with someone who will support you and help you be accountable. Find a friend or coworker who will ask you whether you went for your walk that day or whether you have eaten lunch. Other people can help hold you accountable and help you be successful at practicing self-care. Creating the habit is helpful and will take some time, but once you have created the habit, your self-care activities will be easier to accomplish. It is all about having a plan with concrete goals and then writing down that plan. Make sure your goals are achievable and that they can be measured in some way.

An important component of many of these plans is developing your team of professionals who are going to help you through the process. As discussed in chapter 1, your team can include your divorce lawyer, your therapist, your accountant, your financial adviser, and any other financial experts you may need to help you get through this process. Figure out who these people will be for you, write down their names, and make them part of your plan. Having your team in place can help reduce your stress and take some of the work and worry off your plate. There may be some things the professionals cannot do for you, but once we get the information we need from you, we can start doing the heavy lifting, so you can continue to function in your everyday life. A divorce can be all-consuming, and you may find that while you are going through a divorce, you can't focus on your job or on taking care of your children. Once you have your team in place and are regularly practicing self-care, you can refocus your attention and get back to living your life.

Going through a separation and divorce isn't easy, but ignorance isn't bliss in this situation. Now that you have read this book and have a basic understanding of the process and what you may be entitled to under the law, you are well equipped to take the next step and consult with a lawyer who can further assist you in this journey.

Endnotes

1   *Sorey v. Sorey*, 233 N.C. App. 682,
     757 S.E2d 518 (2014).
2   N.C. Gen. Stat. § 50-16.3A (2019).
3   *Sorey v. Sorey*, 233 N.C. App. 682,
     757 S.E2d 518 (2014).
4   *Hanley v. Hanley*, 128 N.C. App.
     54, 493 S.E.2d 337 (1997).
5   N.C. Gen. Stat. § 14-134.3 (2019).
6   John M. Gottman, PhD, *Why Marriages Succeed
     or Fail* (New York: Simon & Schuster, 1994).
7   Laurie J. Watson, *Wanting Sex Again: How
     to Rediscover Desire and Heal a Sexless
     Marriage* (New York: Berkley Books, 2012).
8   Mediation discussed in this chapter pertains to
     private mediations paid for by the parties. Parties
     may attempt to negotiate their child custody
     disputes through private mediation; however, N.C.
     Gen. Stat. § 7A-494 also establishes a Custody
     and Visitation Mediation program that is a free,
     statewide, custody mediation program required
     for custody claims filed in North Carolina. Parties
     can ask that custody mediation through the court
     system be waived, but it is required in most cases.
9   N.C. Gen. Stat. § 52-10 (2019).
10   Dispute Resolution Commission, www.nccourts.
     gov/commissions/dispute-resolution-commission.

11 N.C. Gen. Stat. § 50-13.7 (2019).

12 C. M. Kamp Dush, L. E. Kotila, and S. J Schoppe-Sullivan, "Predictors of Supportive Coparenting after Relationship Dissolution among At-Risk Parents," *Journal of Family Psychology 25, no. 3 (2011): 356–365.*

13 Kamp Dush, "Predictors of Supportive Coparenting," 356–365.

14 For a brief review of literature, see C. Buckley, "Co-parenting after divorce: Opportunities and challenges," *Clinical Science Insights* (Web article), February 28, 2013. Retrieved from https:// www.family-institute.org/sites/default/files/pdfs/ csi_buckley_co-parenting_after_divorce.pdf; cf. L. Nielsen, "Reexamining the research on parental conflict, co-parenting, and custody arrangements," *Psychol, Public Policy, and Law* 23, no. 2 (May 2017): 211-231, http://dx.doi.org/10.1037/law0000109.

15 Buckley, "Co-parenting after divorce."

16 See, generally, J. Weaver and S. Thomas, "Mediation and Moderation of Divorce Effects on Children's Behavior Problems," *Journal of Family Psychology* 29, no. 1 (November 2014): 39-48. See also P. Amato, "The Consequence of divorce for adults and children," *Journal of Marriage and Family* 62, no. 4 (November 2000): 1269-1287; P. Amato, "Research on Divorce: Continuing trends and new developments," *Journal of Marriage and Family* 72, no. 3 (June 2010): 650-655, http:// dx.doi.org/10.1111/j.1741-3737.2010.00723.x.

17 See, e.g., J. Song and B. Volling, "Coparenting and Children's Temperament Predict Firstborns' Cooperation in the Care of an Infant Sibling," *Journal of Family Psychology* 29, no. 1 (2015): 130-135. http://dx.doi.org/10.1037/fam0000052.

18 N.C. Gen. Stat. § 1A-1, Rule 26 (2019).

19 N.C. Gen. Stat. § 1A-1, Rule 30 (2019).

20 M.F. Faces, T.C. Harford, G.D. Williams, and E.Z. Hanna, "Alcohol consumption and divorce rates in the United States," *Journal of Studies on Alcohol* 60, no. 5 (1999): 647-652, https://www.jsad.com/doi/abs/10.15288/jsa.1999.60.647.

21 "Time Together/Supervised Visitation & Exchange," Triangle Family Services, https://tfsnc.org/supervised-visitation-and-exchange/.

22 All Kids 1st Supervised Visitation, https://allkids1st.weebly.com/.

23 *Perdue v. Fuqua*, 195 N.C. App. 583, 673 S.E.2d 145 (2009).

24 *Wellons v. White*, 229 N.C. App. 164, 748 S.E.2d 709 (2013).

25 *Penland v. Harris*, 135 N.C. App. 359, 520 S.E.2d 105 (1999).

26 N.C. Gen. Stat. § 50-93 (2019).

27 N.C. Gen. Stat. § 50-91(a) and (b) (2019).

28 Our Family Wizard, https://www.ourfamilywizard.com/.

29 N.C. Gen. Stat. § 50-97 (2019).

30 *Pataky v. Pataky*, 160 N.C. App. 289, 585 S.E.2d 404 (2003).

31 N.C. Gen. Stat. § 50-11(e) (2019).

32 *Wachovia Bank and Trust v. Wolfe*, 243 N.C. 469, 475, 91 S.E.2d 246, 251 (1956) (quotation omitted).

33 *Miller v. Miller*, 253 N.C. App. 85, 799 S.E.2d 890 (2017).

34 *Jones v. Jones*, 121 N.C. App. 523, 466 S.E.2d 342 (1996).

35 *Haywood v. Haywood*, 106 N.C. App. 91, 415 S.E.2d 565 (1992), rev'd on other grounds, 333 N.C. 342 (1993).

36 *Godley v. Godley*, 110 N.C. App. 99, 429 S.E.2d 382 (1993).

37 N.C. Gen. Stat. § 50-20(a); *McLean v. McLean*, 323 N.C. 543, 545, 374 S.E.2d 376, 378 (1988) (citations omitted); *Goldston v. Goldston*, 159 N.C. App. 180, 182, 582 S.E.2d 685, 686 (2003).

38 *Minter v. Minter*, 111 N.C. App. 321, 326, 432 S.E.2d 720, 724 (quoting *Atkins v. Atkins*, 102 N.C. App. 199, 206, 401 S.E. 2d 784, 787 (1991).

39 See, e.g., *Goldston*, 159 N.C. App. at 182, 582 S.E.2d at 686 (quoting N.C. Gen. Stat. § 50-20 (b)(1) (2001)).

40 *Friend-Novorska v. Novorska*, 131 N.C. App. 508,511, 507 S.E.2d 900, 902 (citing N.C. Gen. Stat. § 50-20(b)(2)).

41 *Minter,* 111 N.C. App. at 327, 432 S.E.2d at 724 (quotation omitted).

42 *Minter*, 111 N.C. App. at 326, 432 S.E.2d at 724 (citation omitted).

43 See *Goldston*, 159 N.C. App. at 183, 582 S.E.2d at 686 (citing Nix v. Nix, 80 N.C. App.

110, 113, 341 S.E.2d 116, 118 (1986)).

44 *Goldston,* 159 N.C. App.at 183, 582 S.E.2d at 687 (citing *Wade v. Wade,* 72 N.C. App. 372, 381-82, 325 S.E.2d 260, 269, disc. review denied, 313 N.C. 612, 330 S.E.2d 616 (1985)).

45 *Goldston,* 159 N.C. App. at 183, 582 S.E.2d at 687 (citations omitted)

46 See, e.g., *Lawrence v. Lawrence,* 75 N.C. App. 592, 595-96, 331 S.E.2d 186, 188 ("[T]hat part of the property consisting of the additions, alterations and repairs provided during marriage should be considered marital in nature." (emphasis in original)), disc. review denied, 314 N.C. 541, 335 S.E.2d 18 (1985).

47 *Hagler v. Hagler,* 319 N.C. 287, 289, 354 S.E.2d 228, 232 (1987).

48 *Wirth v. Wirth,* 193 N.C. App. 657, 661, 668 S.E.2d 603, 607 (2008).

49 *Lund v. Lund,* 7244 N.C. App. 279, 289, 79 S.E.2d 175, 182 (2015).

50 N.C. Gen. Stat. § 50-20(b)(4) (2019).

51 Cheryl Howell, "Equitable Distribution: Divisible Property and Burdens of Proof," *On the Civil Side: A UNC School of Government Blog,* September 22, 2017, https://civil.sog.unc.edu/equitable-distribution-divisible-property-and-burdens-of-proof/.

52 *Walter v. Walter,* 149 N.C. App. 723, fn2, 561 S.E.2d 571, fn2 (2002).

53 *Lund,* 252 N.C. App. 306, 798 S.E.2d 424.

54 N.C. Gen. Stat. § 50-20 (2019).

55 *White v. White*, 312 N.C. 770, 776, 324 S.E.2d 829, 832 (1985).

56 N.C. Gen. Stat. § 50-20(b)(3) (2019). "Distributive award" means a payment made by one spouse to the other for purposes of equalizing the marital estate between the parties.

57 N.C. Gen. Stat. § 50-16.1A (2019).

58 N.C. Gen. Stat. § 50-16.2A (2019).

59 N.C. Gen. Stat. § 50-16.2A (2019).

60 N.C. Gen. Stat. § 50-16.1A (2019).

61 N.C. Gen. Stat. § 50B-1 (2019).

62 N.C. Gen. Stat. § 50B-3.1 (2019).

63 N.C. Gen. Stat. § 50C-1(6) (2019).

About the Author

Jaime H. Davis is a North Carolina board-certified family law specialist and partner in the family law firm Gailor Hunt Jenkins Davis Taylor & Gibbs, PLLC in Raleigh, North Carolina. Jaime graduated from the University of North Carolina at Chapel Hill in 1998 with a bachelor's in political science and English. She attended law school at the University of North Carolina School of Law receiving her law degree in 2001. Jaime's practice incorporates all areas of family law, with a concentration in complex equitable distribution and child custody matters, including relocation and interstate cases. Jaime also focuses on family law contracts, including premarital, postnuptial, and separation agreements and property settlements. Jaime is a certified parenting coordinator and has been certified by the North Carolina Dispute Resolution Commission as a family financial mediator. She was selected to Super Lawyers in 2019 and was named a Super Lawyers Rising Star in 2013–2016. Jaime was also named to

Business North Carolina's Legal Elite in Family Law in 2018 and 2019. Jaime formerly served as chair of the Wake County Bar Association's Poverty Issues Committee. She currently serves as an attorney volunteer for the UNC Chapel Hill Community Legal Project and The Child's Advocate. Jaime was named to the North Carolina Pro Bono Honor Society in 2018. Jaime lives in Raleigh with her husband and three children.

Additional Resources

Throughout the book, guests who appeared on the *A Year and a Day* podcast were credited for sharing their expertise. Thank you to each of them for their assistance and expertise. Below, you can read a little more about their credentials and the services they provide to individuals, couples, and families undergoing separation and divorce.

Melissa Essick is a board-certified family law specialist and attorney with Gailor Hunt Jenkins Davis Taylor & Gibbs, PLLC. She also is professionally trained as a mediator in all family law matters and certified as a family financial mediator by the North Carolina Dispute Resolution Commission. Melissa currently serves on the Board of Directors for the Foundation for Good Business, a nonprofit organization that provides educational scholarships to children in need, and as a panel advisor for Athena Powerlink, a national mentoring program that connects selected women business owners with a skilled advisory panel for greater success. Melissa earned her bachelor's from the University of North Carolina at Wilmington and her law degree from Campbell University.

Stephanie Gibbs is a North Carolina board-certified family law specialist, certified family financial mediator, and partner in the law firm Gailor Hunt Jenkins Davis Taylor & Gibbs, PLLC. Before joining Gailor Hunt, Stephanie was a criminal defense attorney and also served as a law clerk to the Honorable Martha A. Geer at the North Carolina Court of Appeals. In addition to representing clients in family law matters, Stephanie offers representation in criminal matters that may arise in domestic cases. Stephanie graduated magna cum laude from the State University of New York College at Brockport with a bachelor's in English and written communication. After working more than twenty years as an award-winning journalist, Stephanie received her law degree from the University of North Carolina Law School at Chapel Hill.

Katie Hardersen King is a North Carolina board-certified family law specialist, certified parenting coordinator, and partner at Wake Family Law Group (Sokol Schilawski O'Shaughnessy Grace King & Mauney, PLLC) in Raleigh. Her practice consists exclusively of family law, appeals, surrogacy, and parent coordination. She is a frequent speaker and writer on family law topics and served on the committee that helped draft the 2019 revisions for the state's parenting coordinator statutes. She earned her bachelor's in English and political studies from Meredith College and her law degree from Campbell University School of Law.

Caroline Byrd Landen is the clinical manager at Awakenings Counseling and the clinical director at Counseling Near Me. She specializes in relationships—those with our partners, families, God, and oneself. She has specialized training in trauma and trauma recovery, sex therapy, attachment theory and the practice of attachment, and emotionally focused therapy. She is currently working on completing her license in Christian sex therapy. Caroline completed her undergraduate degree in psychology from North Carolina State University and her graduate degree in marriage and family therapy at the University of Southern Mississippi.

Lynn Wilson McNally is a partner in the law firm Smith Debnam Narron Drake Saintsing & Myers, LLP, and co-leader of the firm's family law practice group. She is a North Carolina board-certified family law specialist and is certified by the North Carolina Dispute Resolution Commission to conduct mediations of equitable distribution and other family financial cases. She represents individuals in matters involving separation, divorce, child custody, child support, alimony, equitable distribution, domestic violence, termination of parental rights, legitimation, and other matters pertaining to family law. She earned her bachelor's from the University of North Carolina at Chapel Hill and her law degree from Campbell University.

Jonathan Melton is a North Carolina board-certified family law specialist and partner in the firm Gailor Hunt Jenkins Davis Taylor & Gibbs, PLLC. Prior to joining Gailor Hunt, Jonathan served as a judicial law clerk for the Honorable Richard A. Elmore of the North Carolina Court of Appeals. Jonathan was a chapter editor of the second edition of the *North Carolina Family Law Case Book* and has presented at continuing legal education seminars on family law-related topics. Jonathan graduated from the honors program of North Carolina State University with a bachelor's in political Science and earned his law degree from North Carolina Central University.

Nicole Taylor is a family lawyer and partner in the firm Gailor Hunt Jenkins Davis Taylor & Gibbs, PLLC. She is professionally trained as a mediator in all family law matters and certified as a family financial mediator by the North Carolina Dispute Resolution Commission. Her practice is concentrated primarily in the area of complex equitable distribution litigation. Nicole graduated magna cum laude from East Carolina University with a bachelor's in political science and earned her law degree from the University of North Carolina at Chapel Hill.

Lori C. Thomas is the director of forensic services at Wynns Family Psychology, a child and adolescent psychology practice located in North Carolina, with offices in Cary and North Raleigh. She provides psychotherapy to children and their families, conducts private and court-ordered psychological evaluations and custody evaluations, works with high-conflict families, and is a trained parent coordinator. Her professional experience includes working with victims of domestic violence, treating eating disorders, and mediating divorce and custody issues. She holds a doctorate in clinical psychology from Drexel University and a law degree from Villanova University.

Carrie Tortora is a North Carolina board-certified family law specialist and partner in the law firm Gailor Hunt Jenkins Davis Taylor & Gibbs, PLLC. Before joining Gailor Hunt, Carrie served as a law clerk to the Honorable Sanford L. Steelman, Jr. of the North Carolina Court of Appeals. Carrie has a background in accounting, which has enabled her to develop an expertise in complex financial cases, such as valuing and dividing business interests, analyzing property distribution, and financial support issues. She also has extensive trial experience with a wide array of family law issues, including custody. She graduated summa cum laude with an accounting degree from Louisiana State University and earned her law degree with honors from the University of North Carolina at Chapel Hill.

If you enjoyed the book, check out full episodes of the podcast. Seasons 1 and 2 of *A Year and a Day: Divorce without Destruction* are available on Apple Podcasts and streaming at divorceistough.com/podcasts.

Still have questions?
Not sure what to do next? Call Jaime Davis at 919.832.8488 to set up an initial consultation.